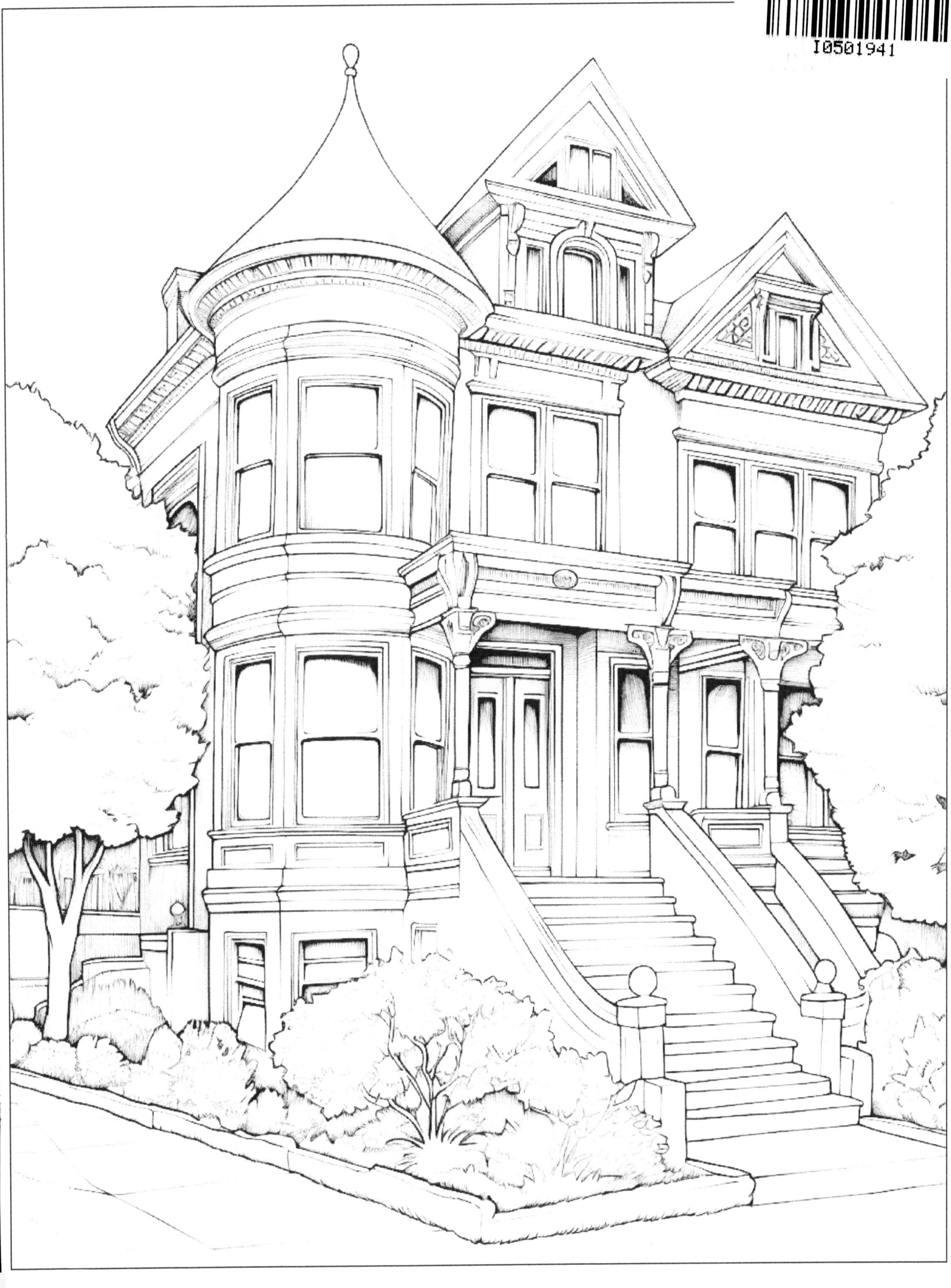

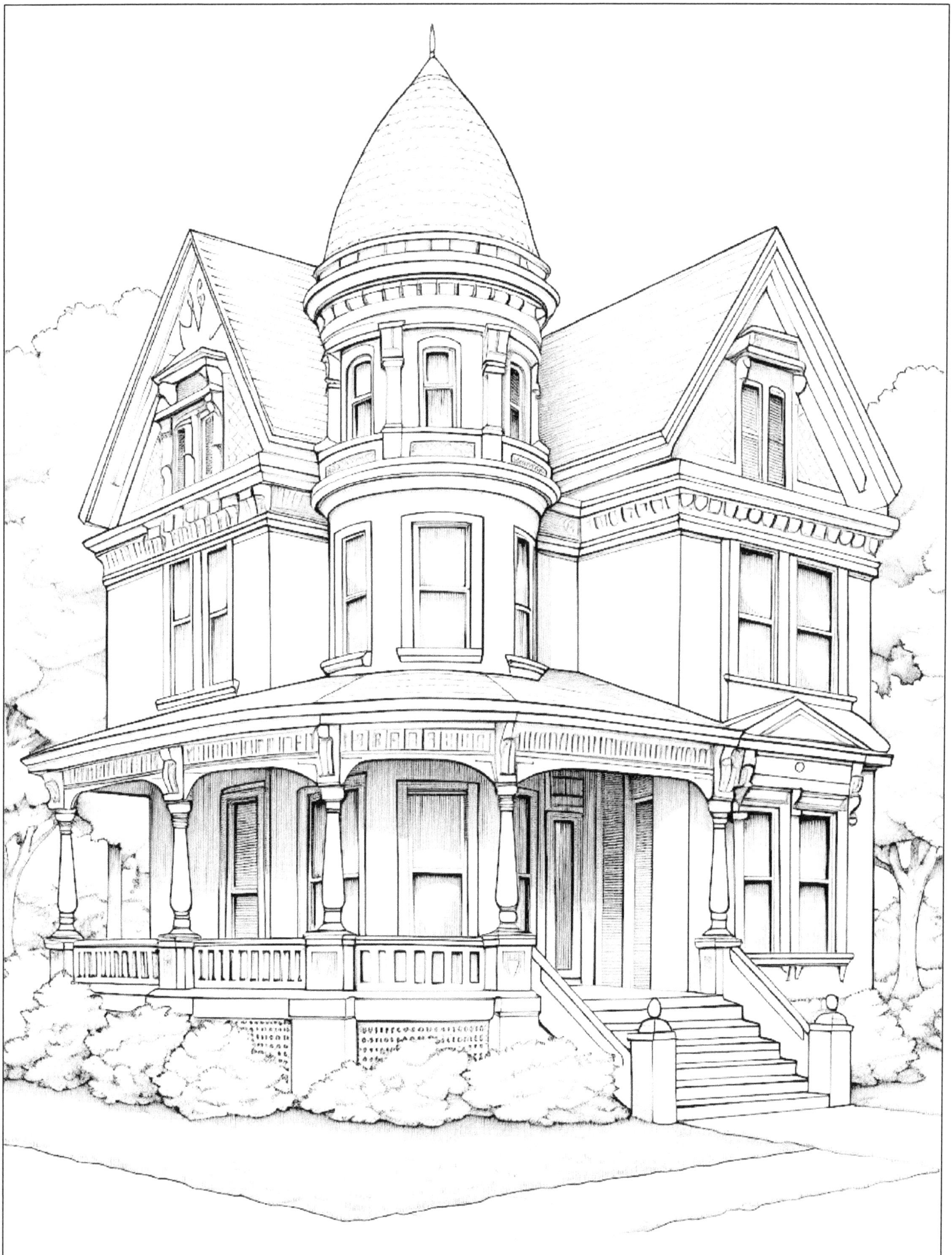

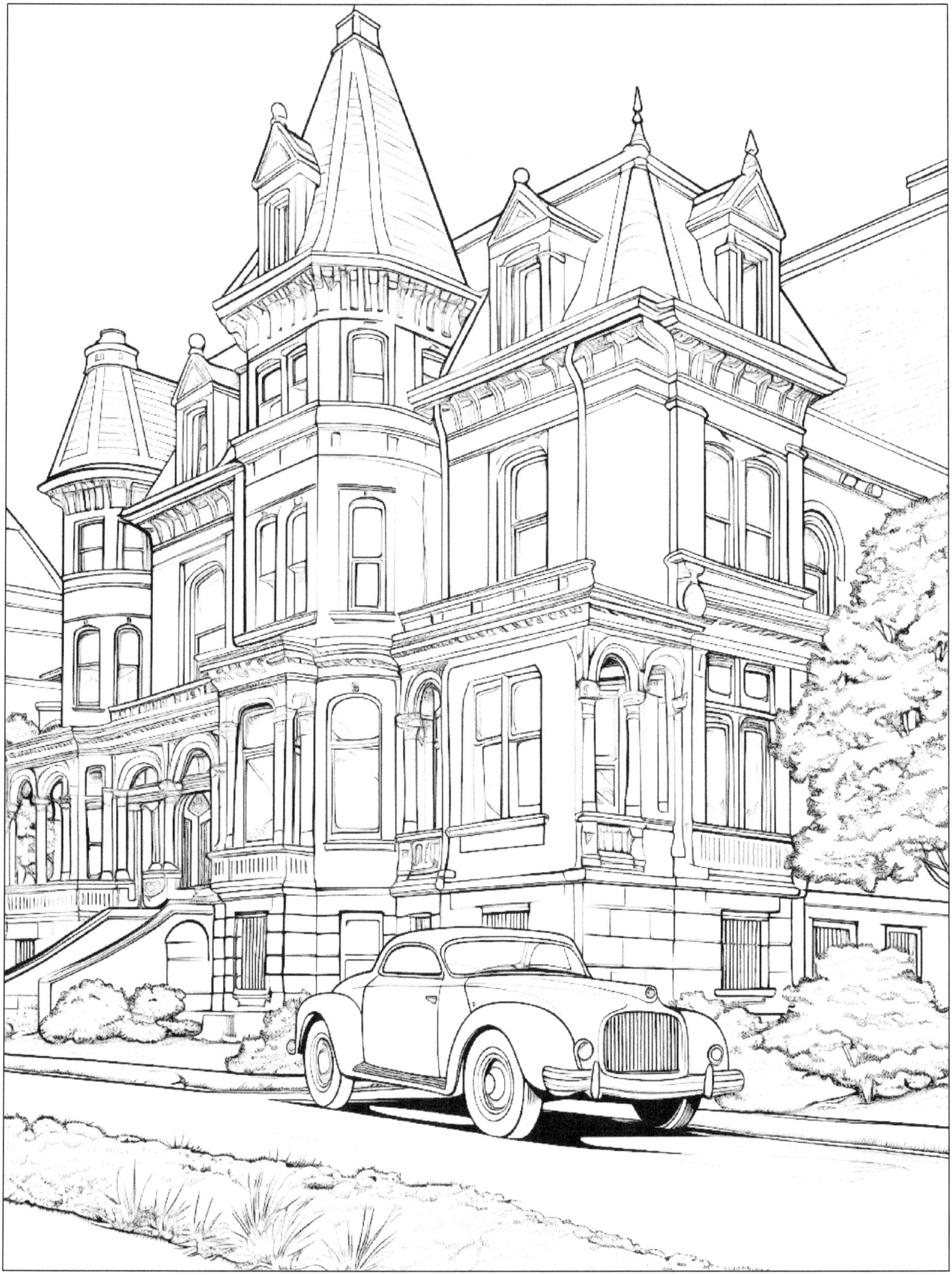

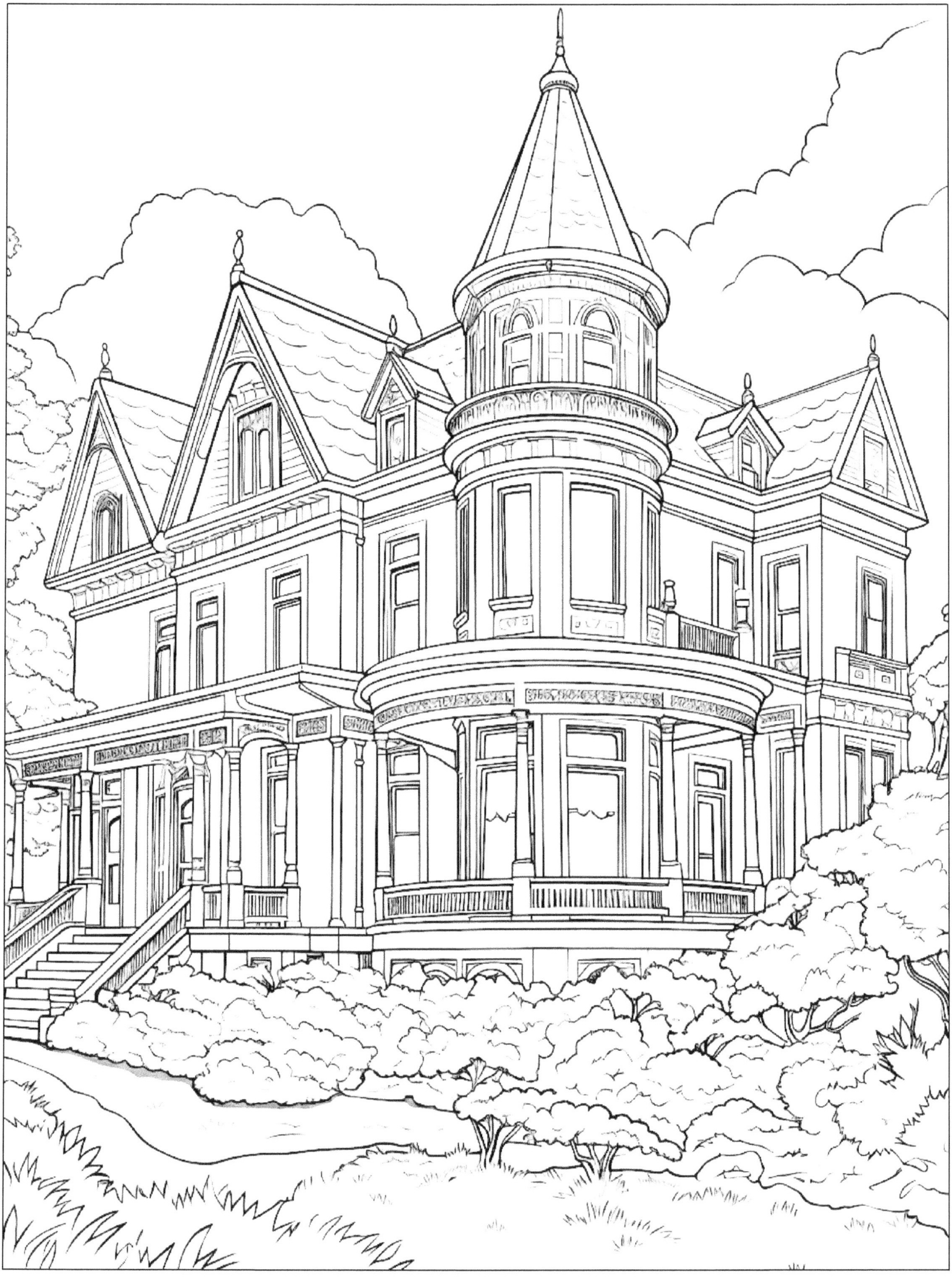

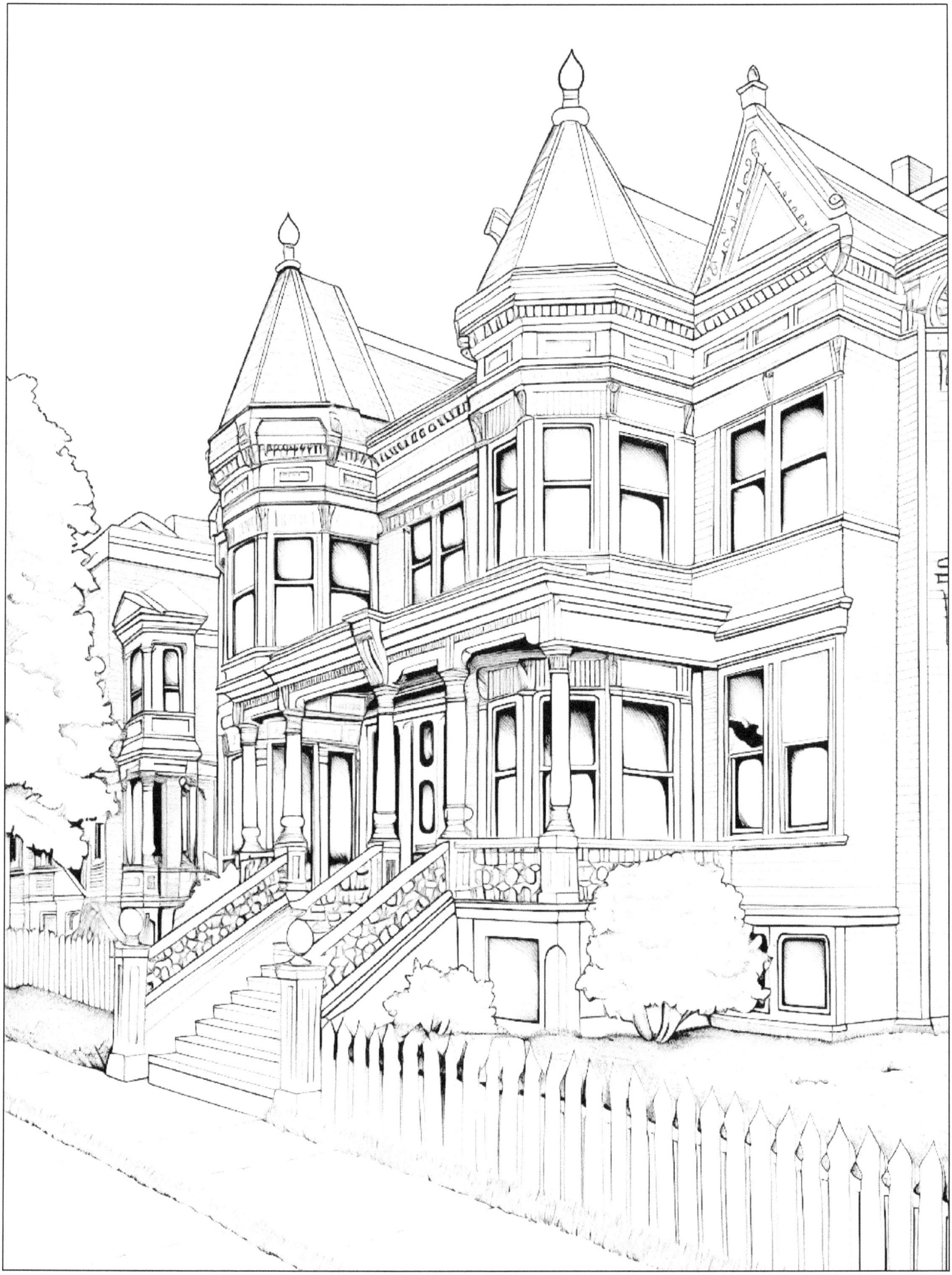

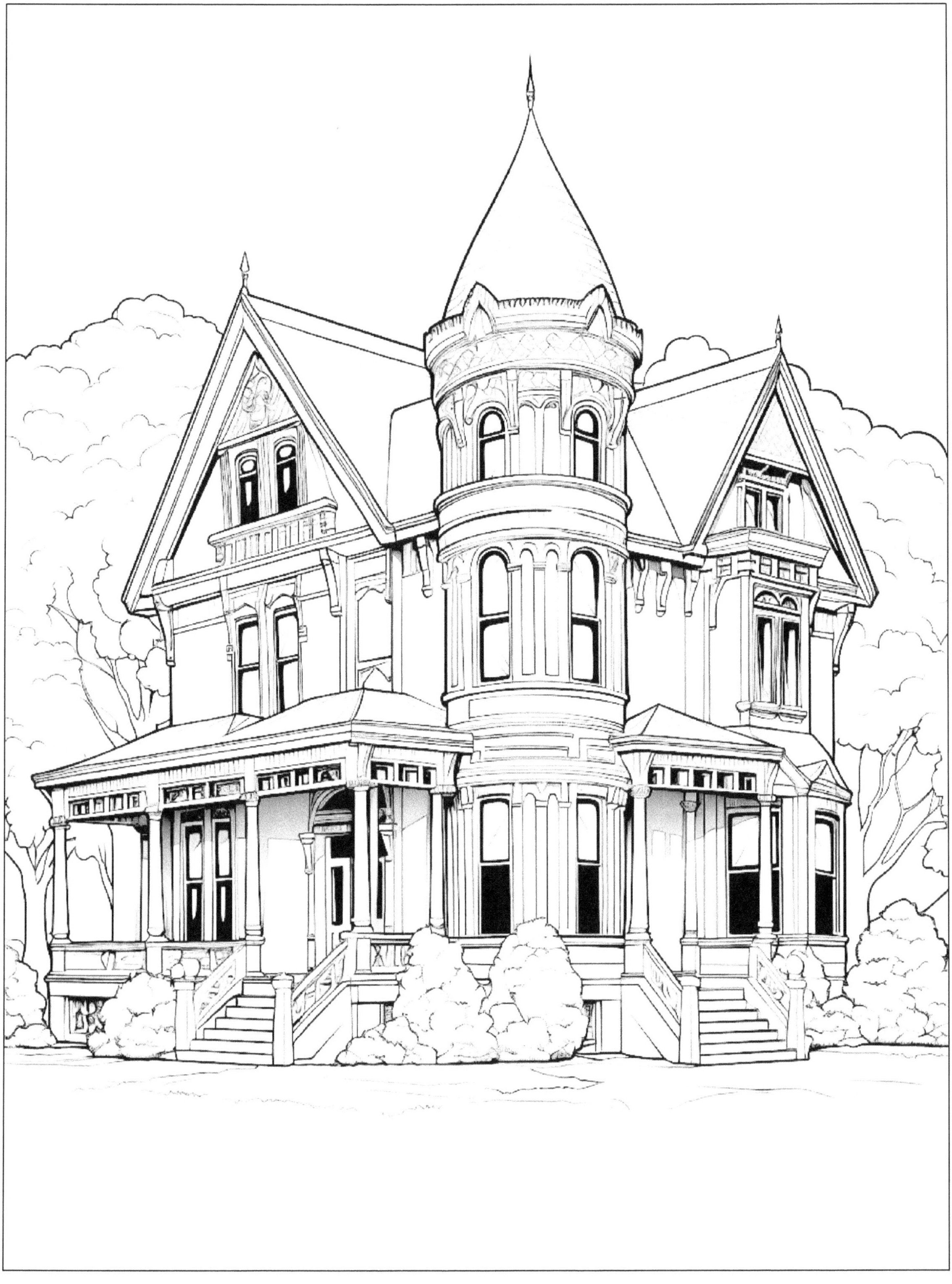

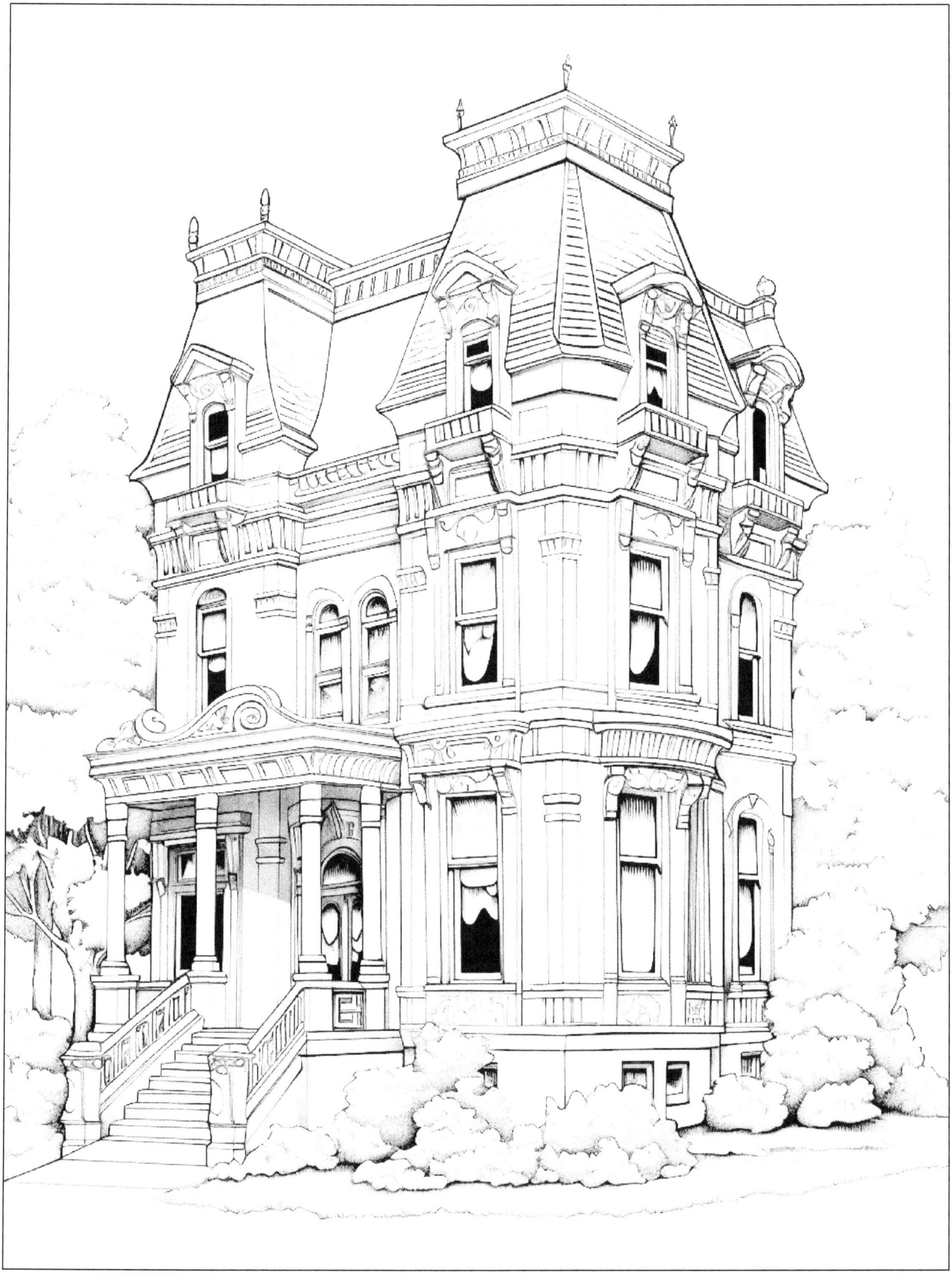

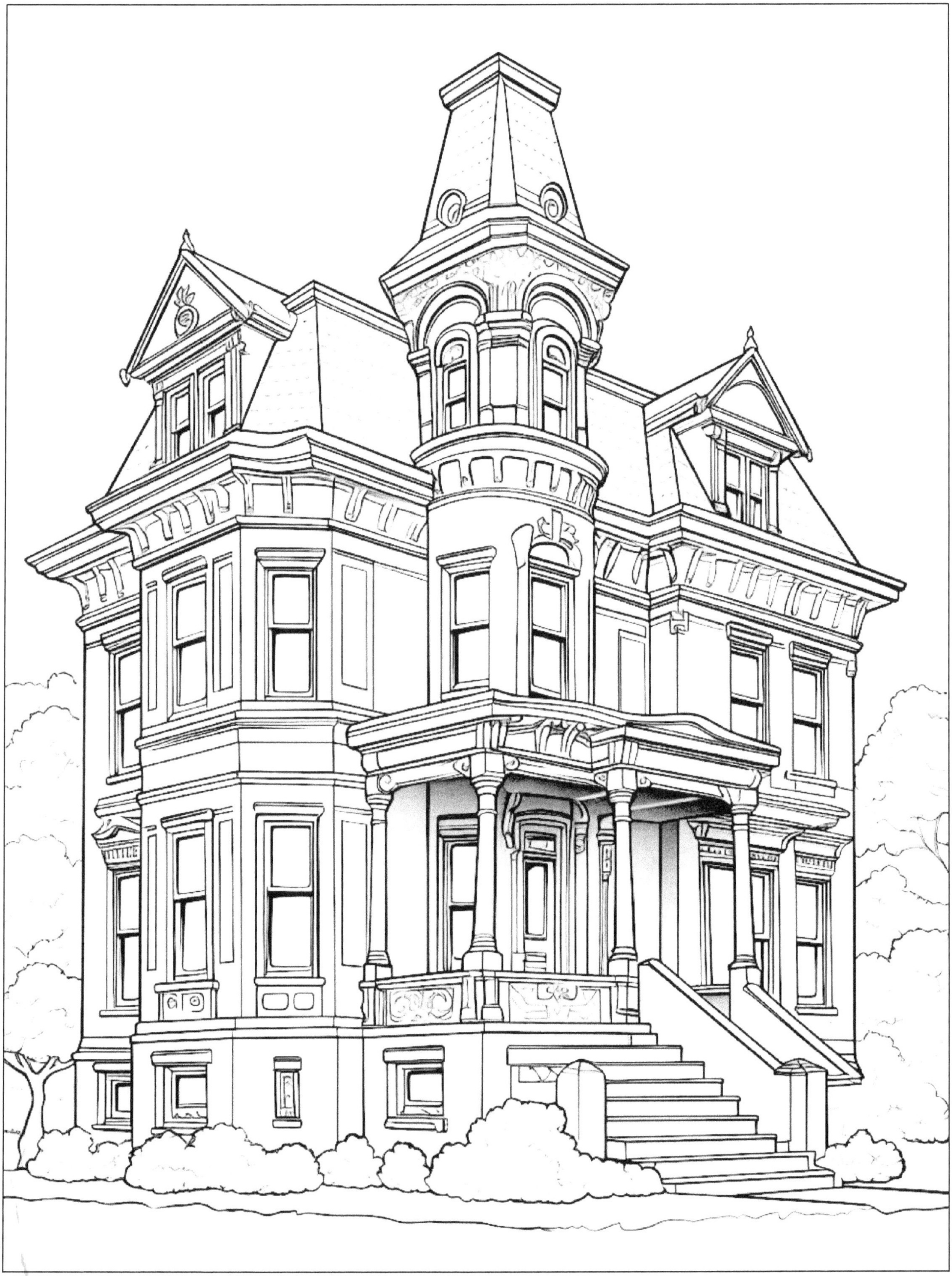

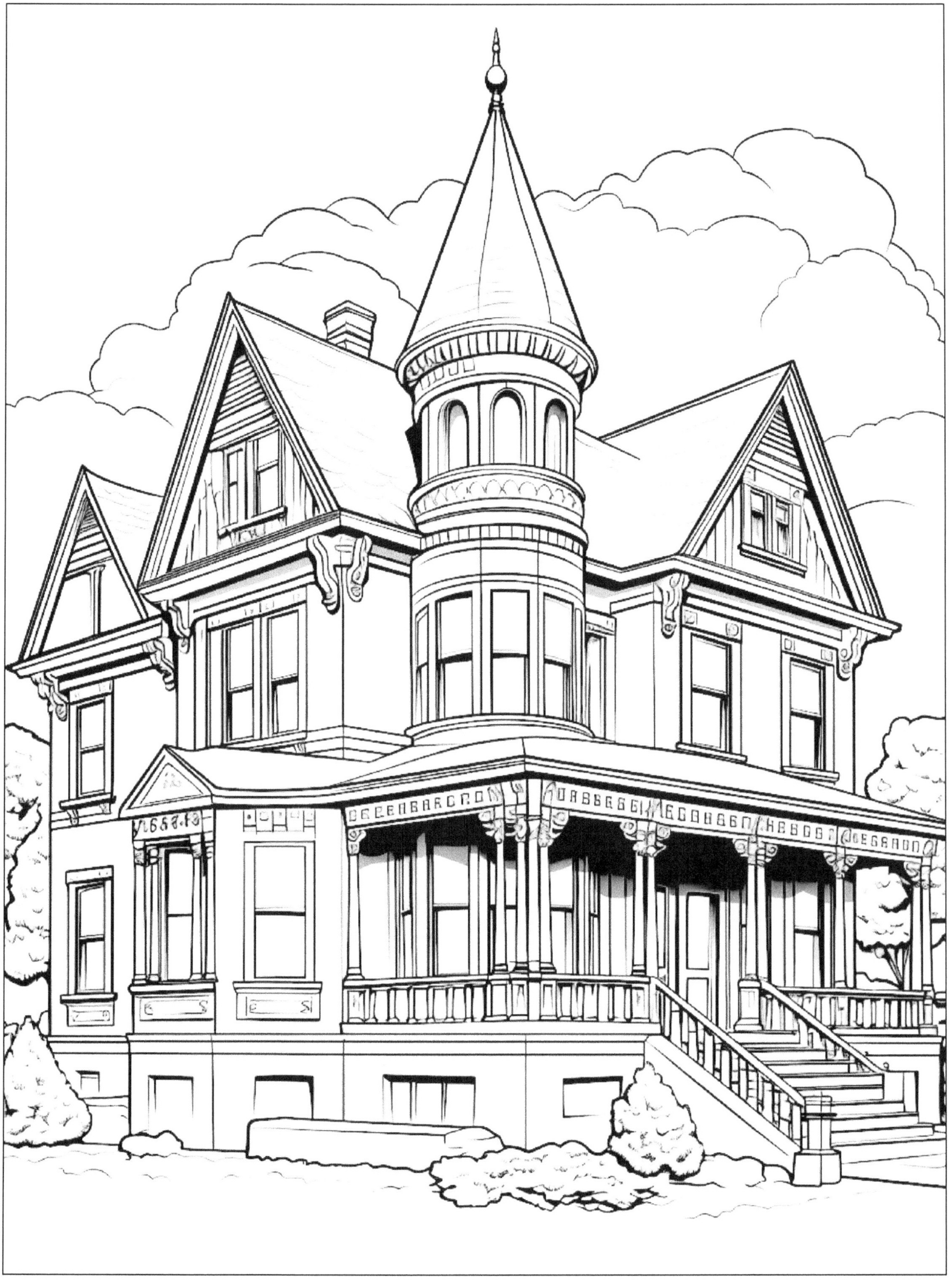

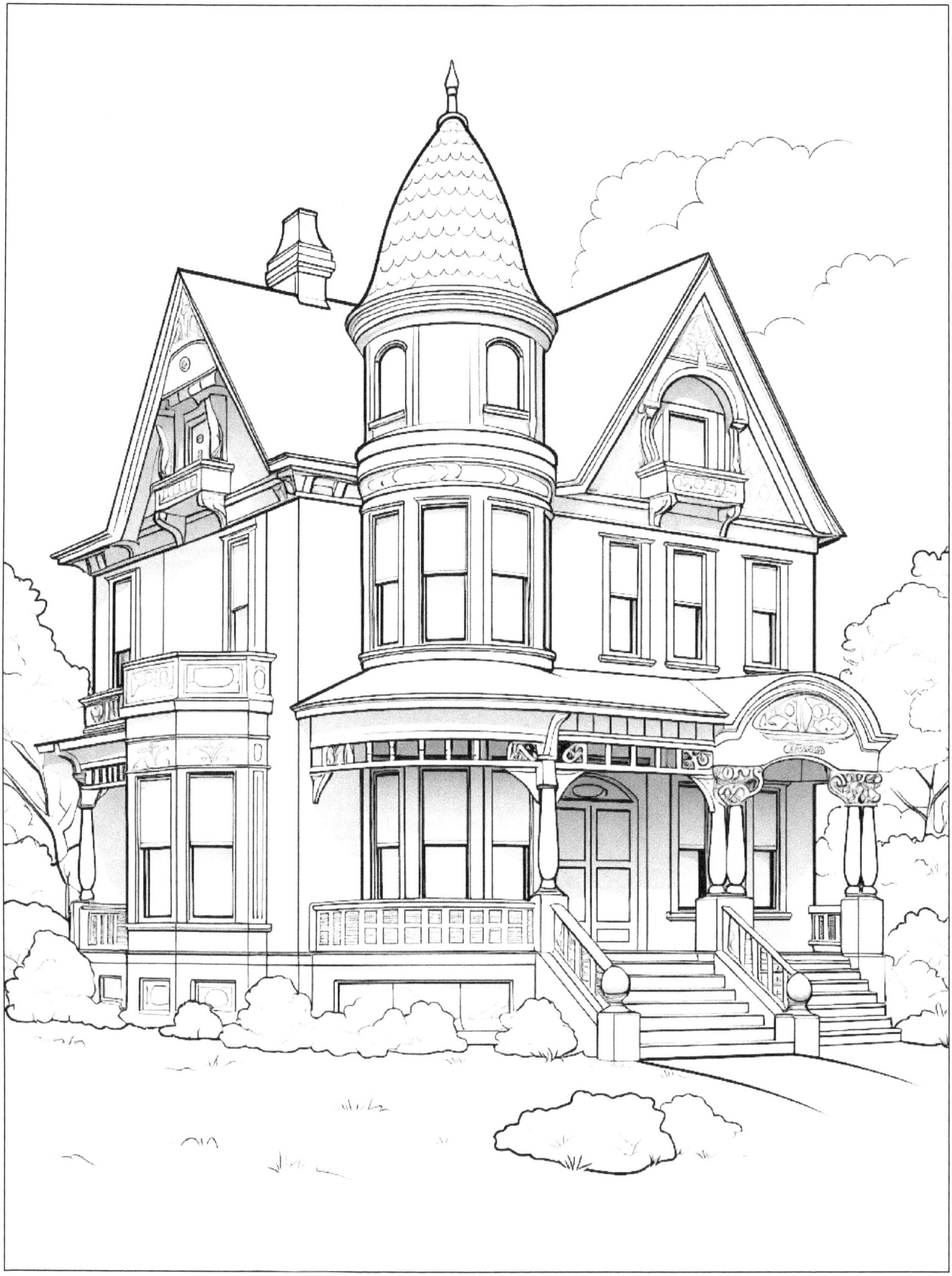

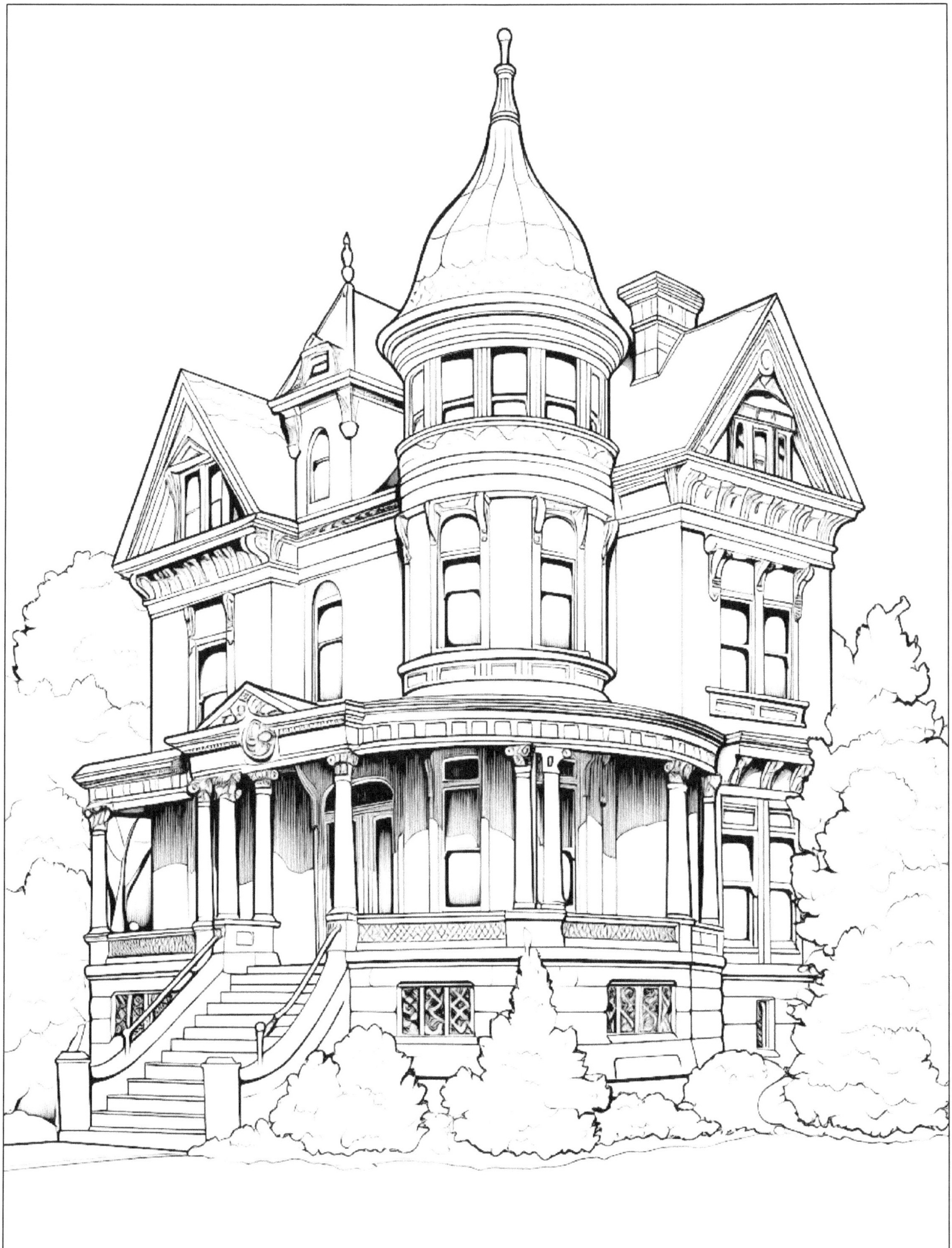

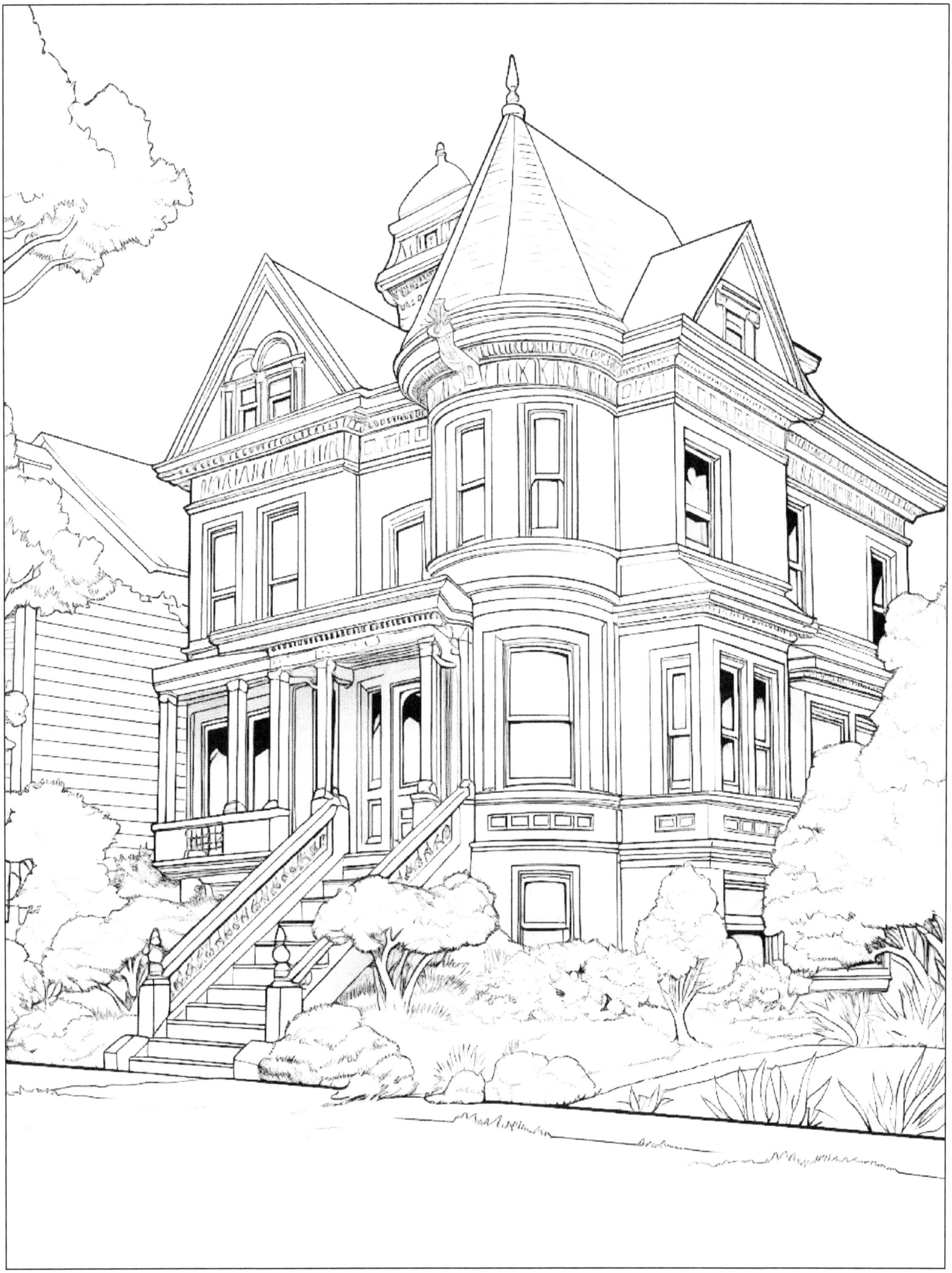

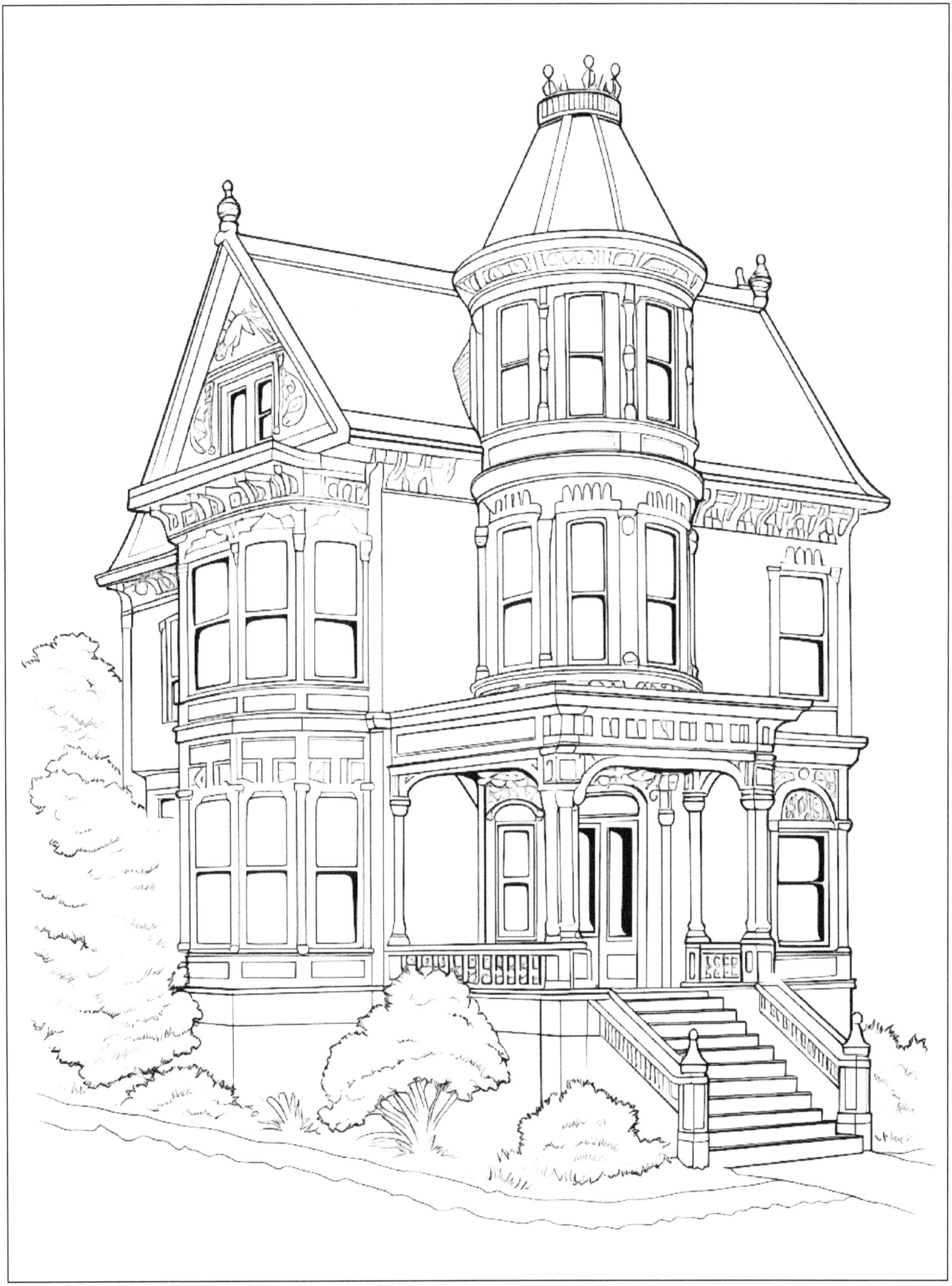

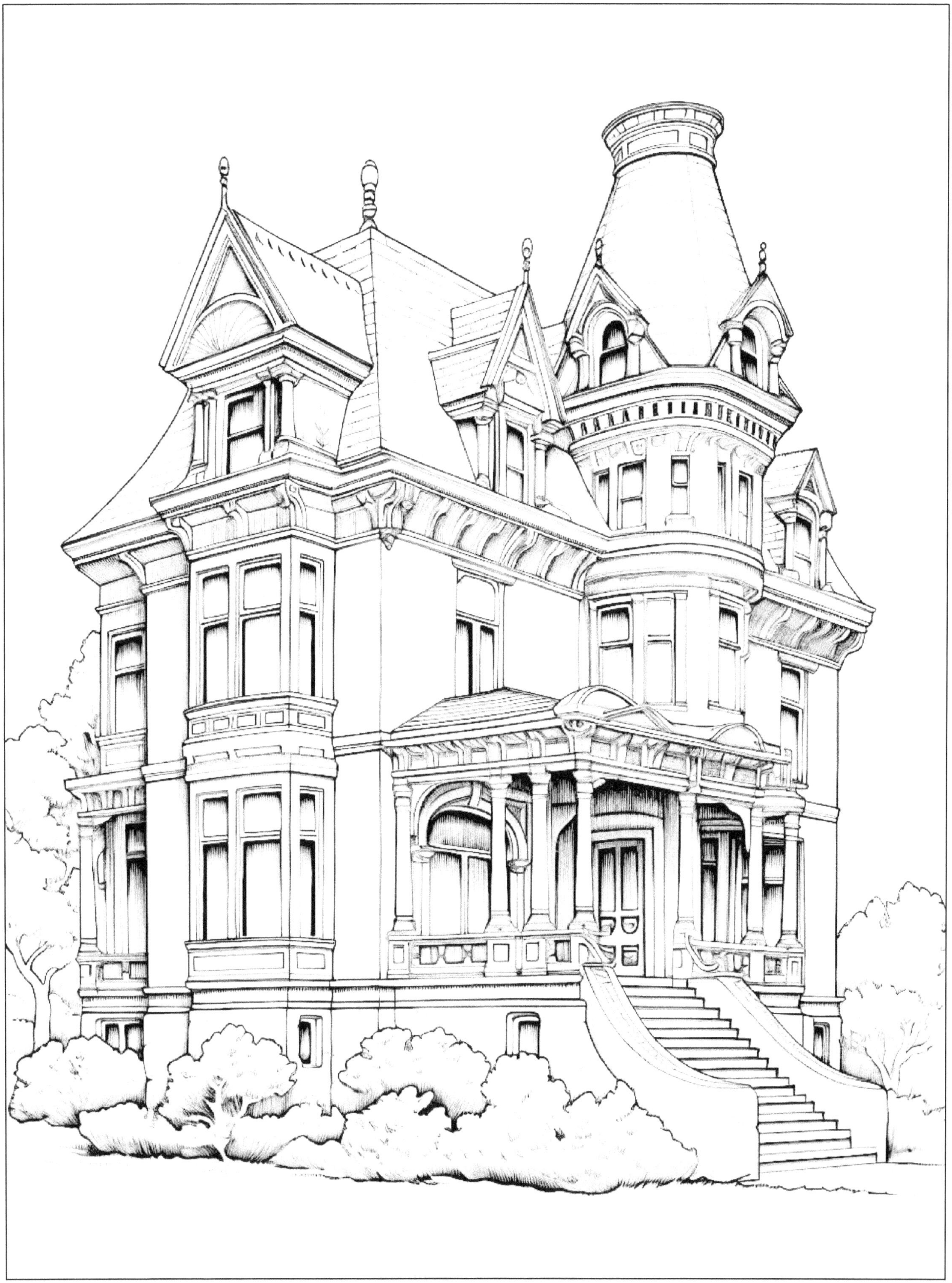

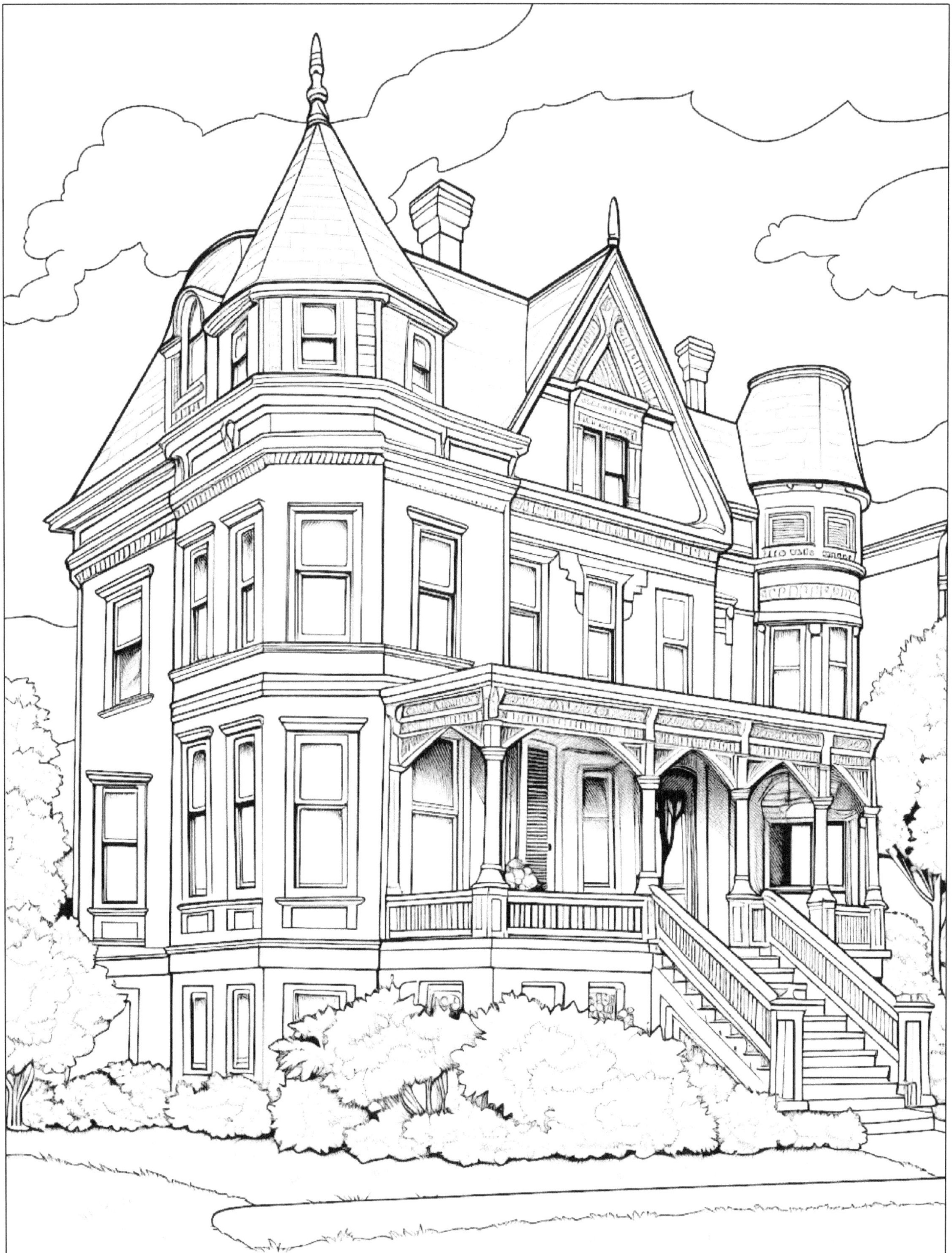

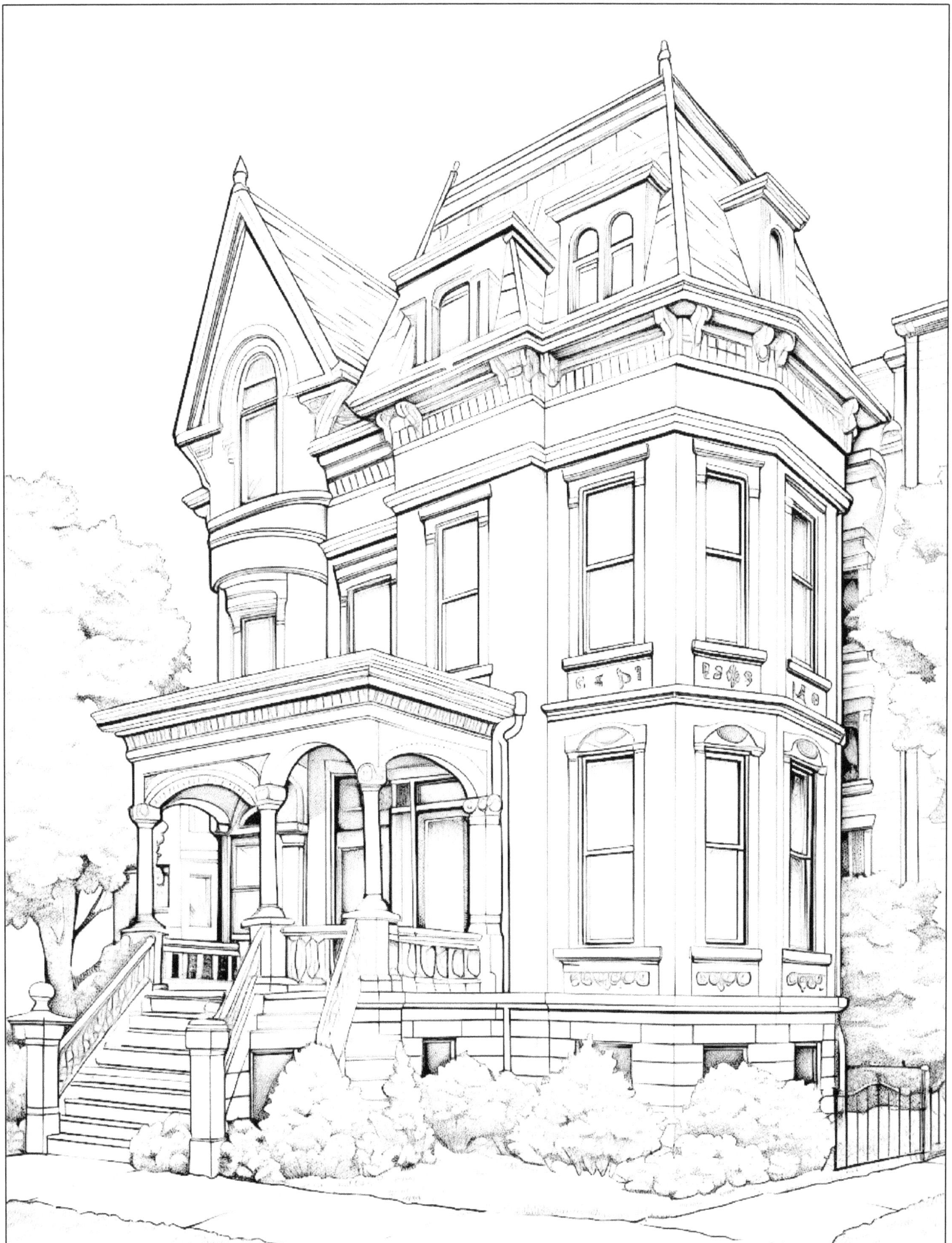

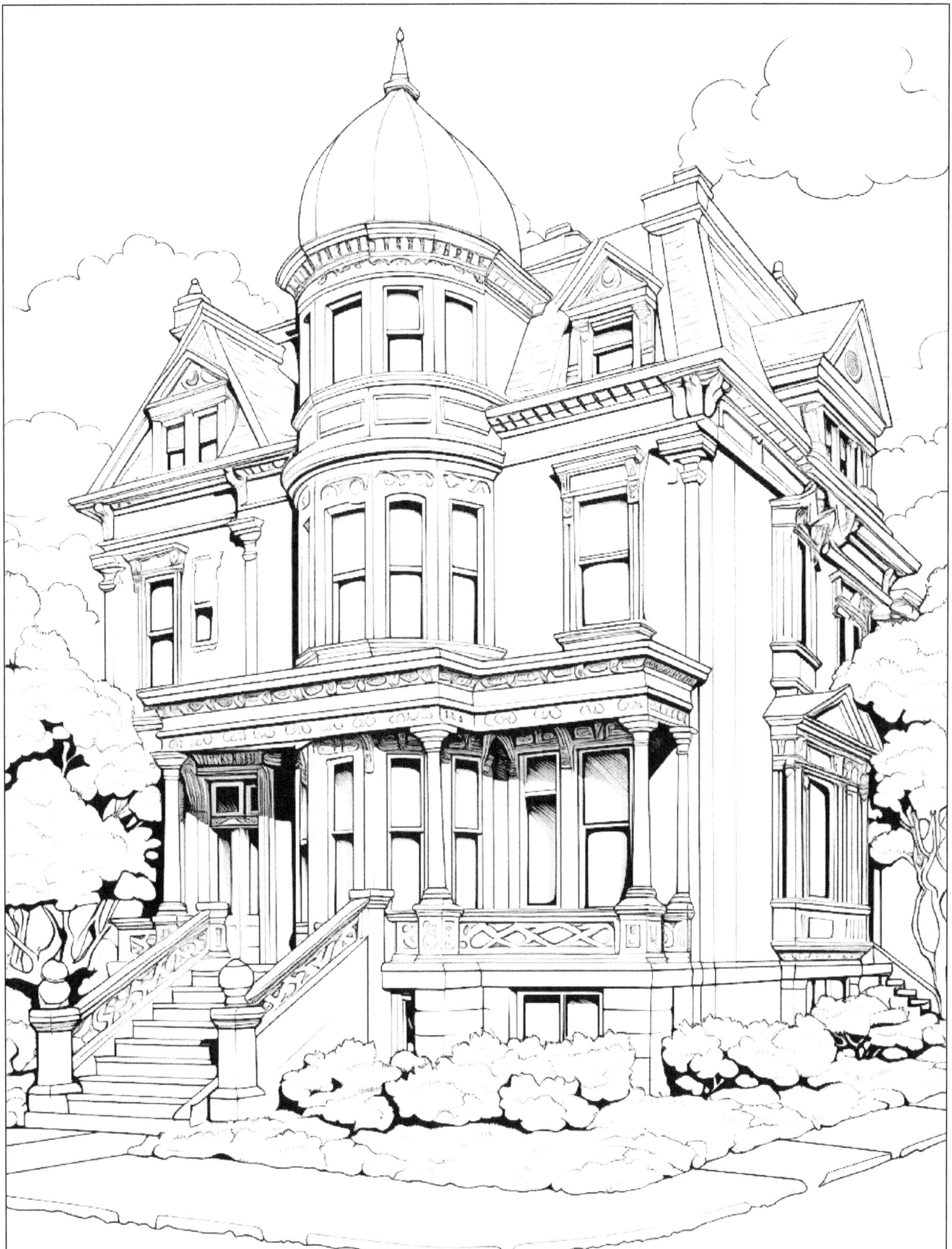

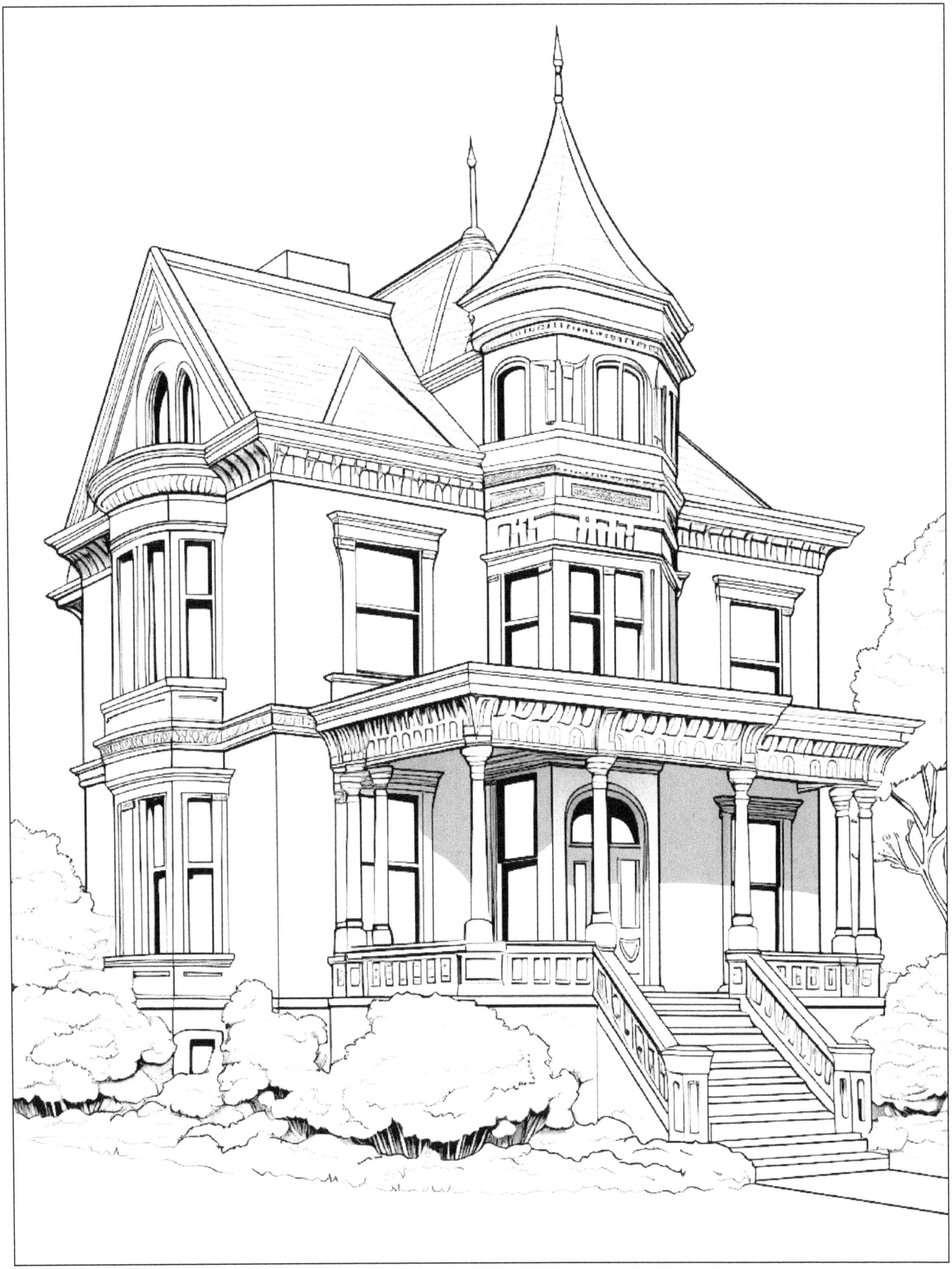

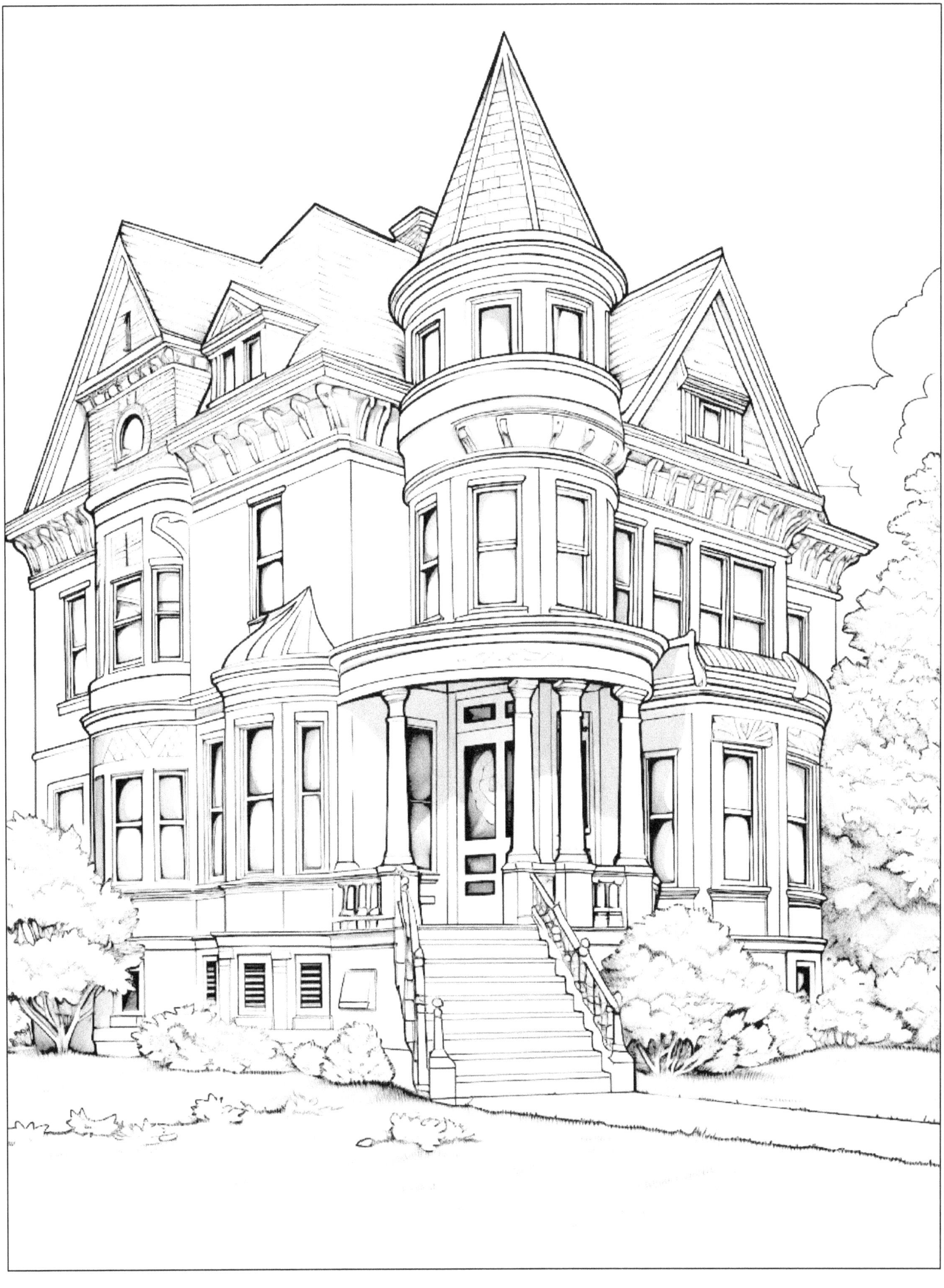

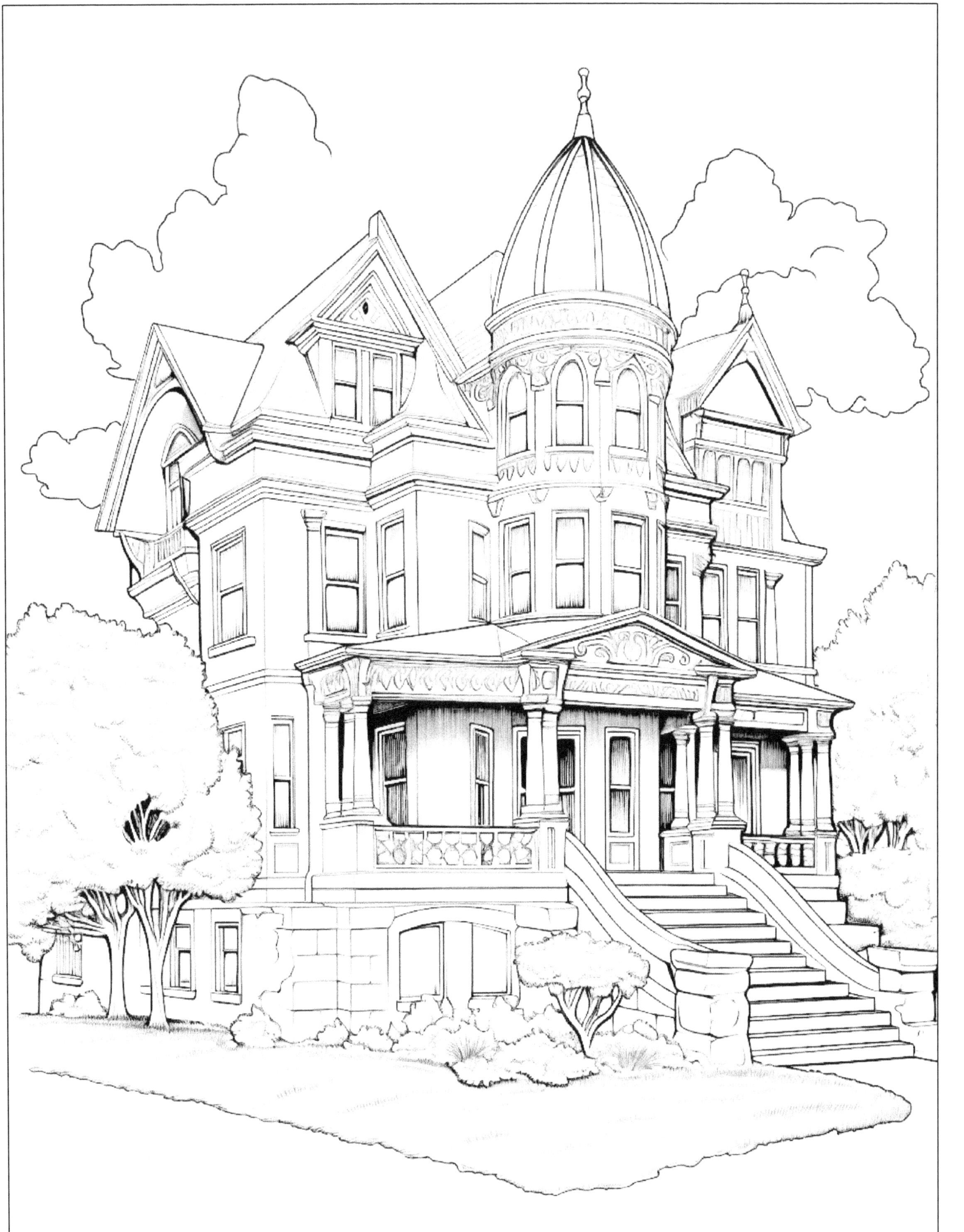

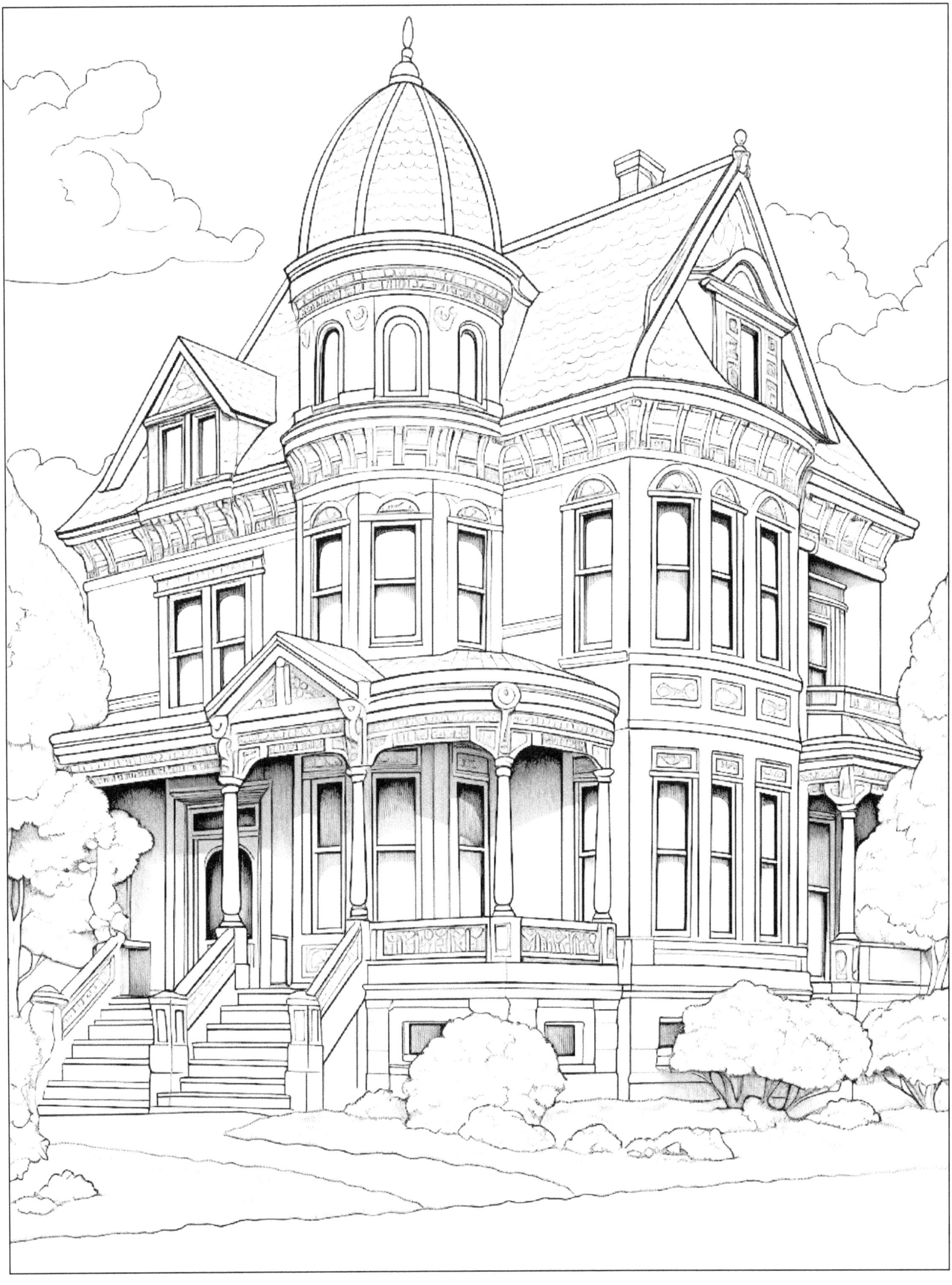

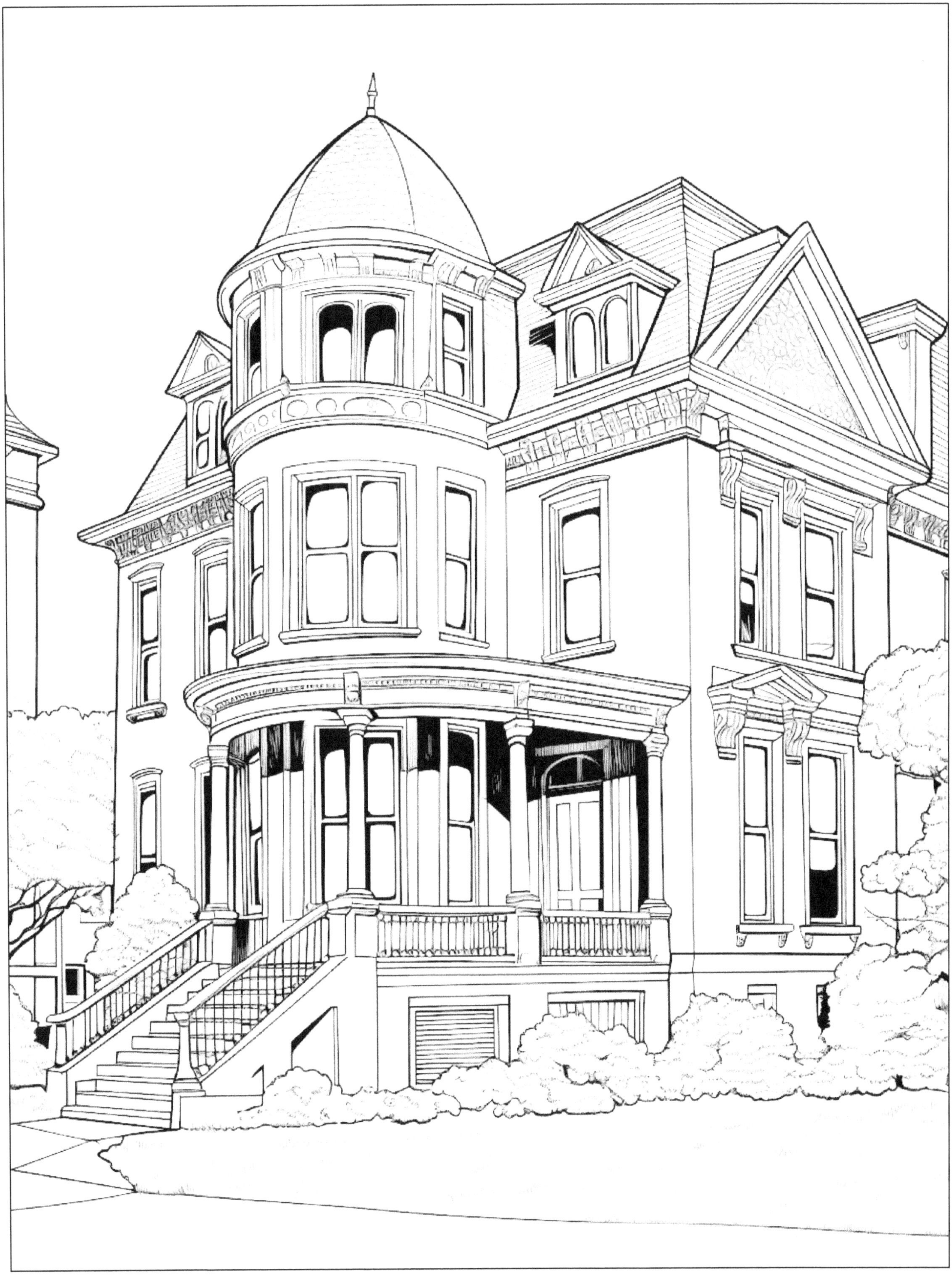

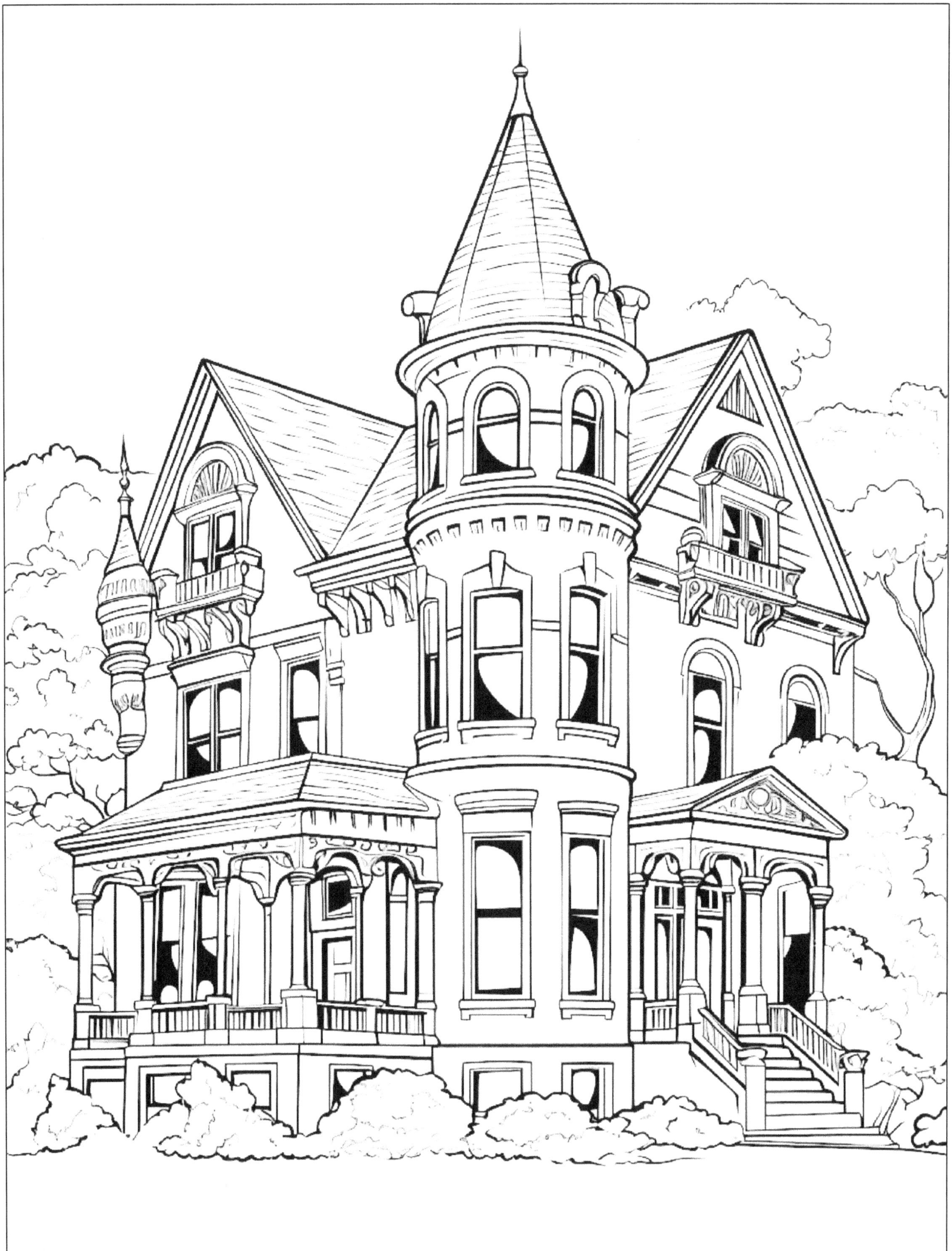

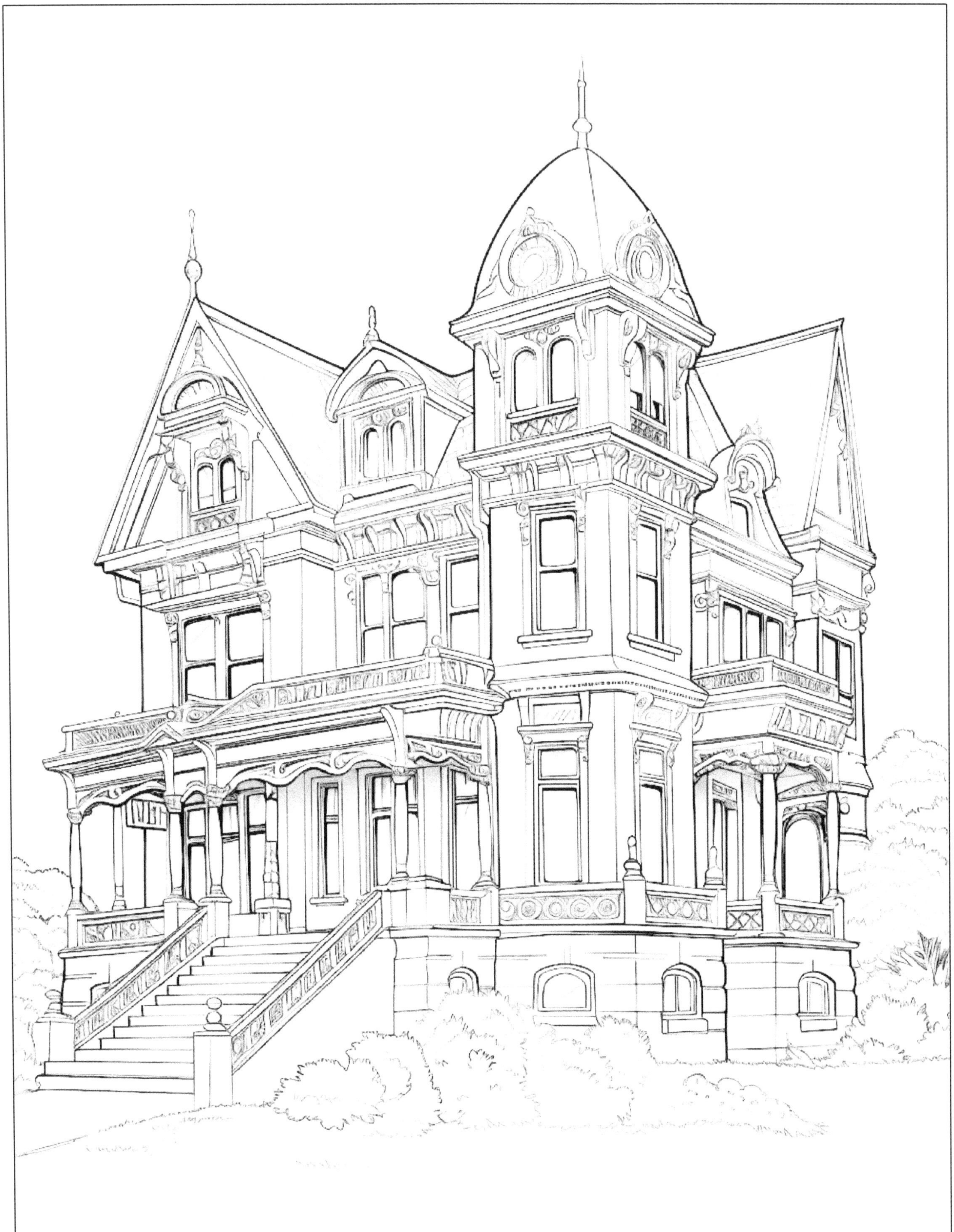

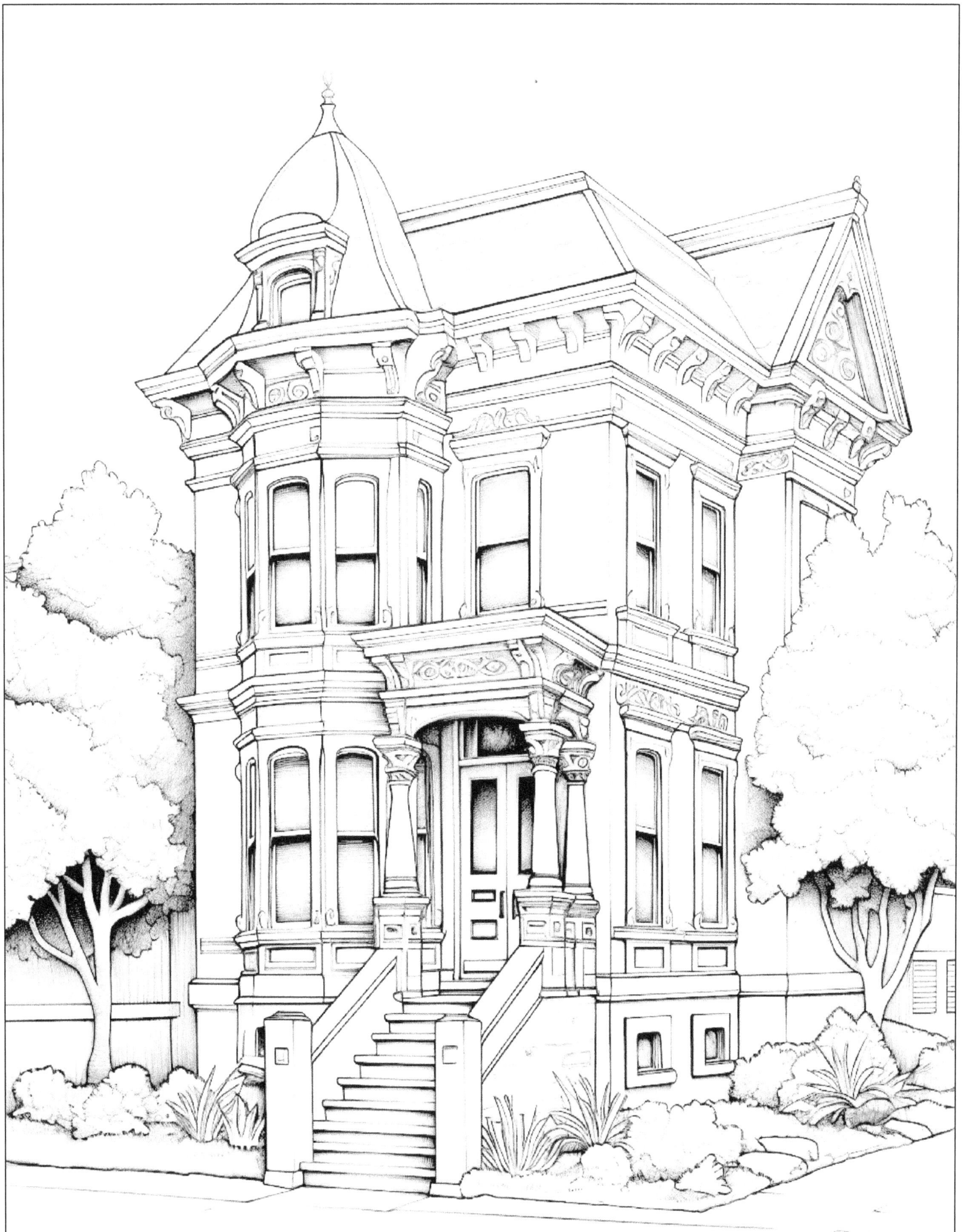

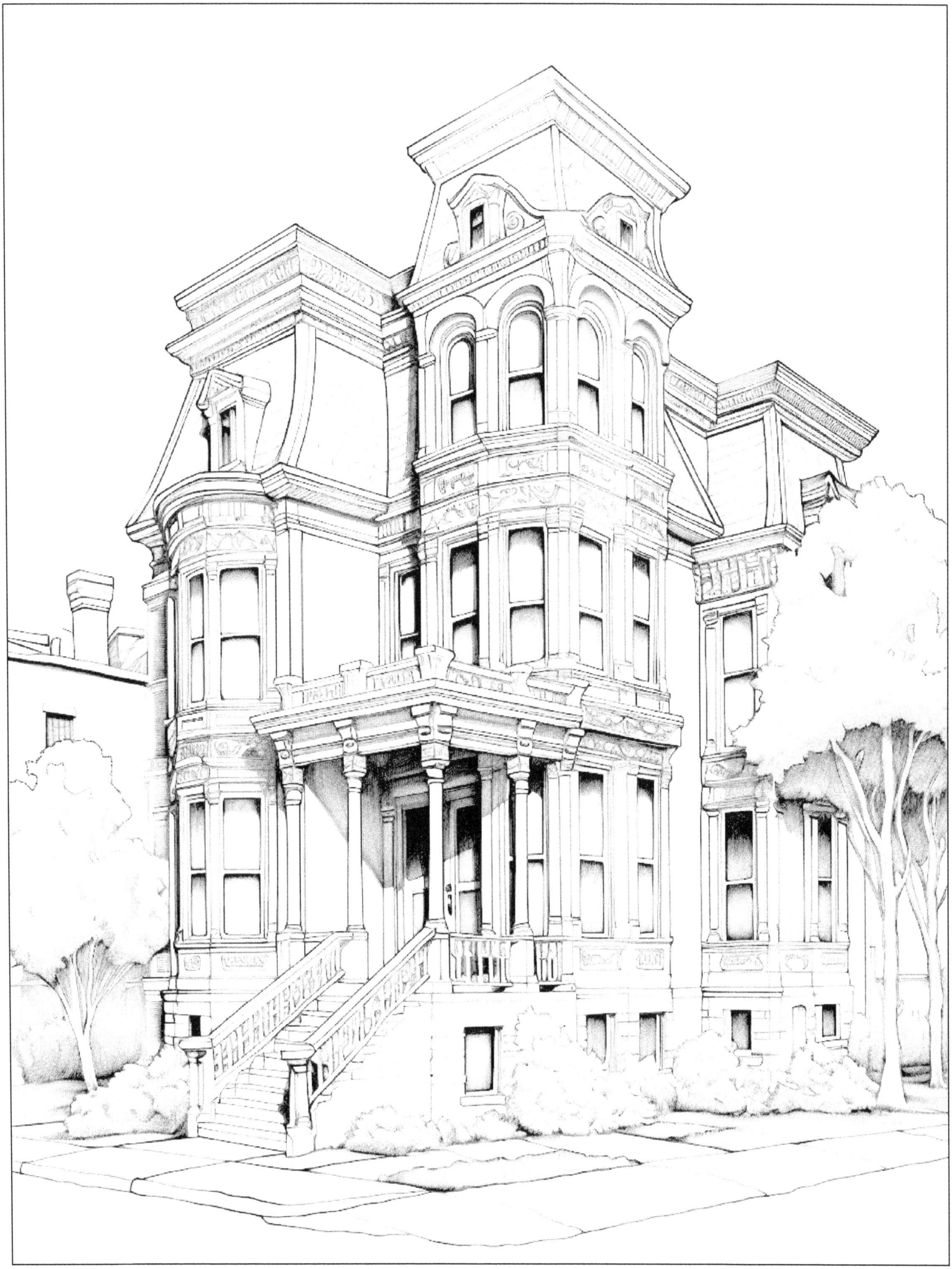

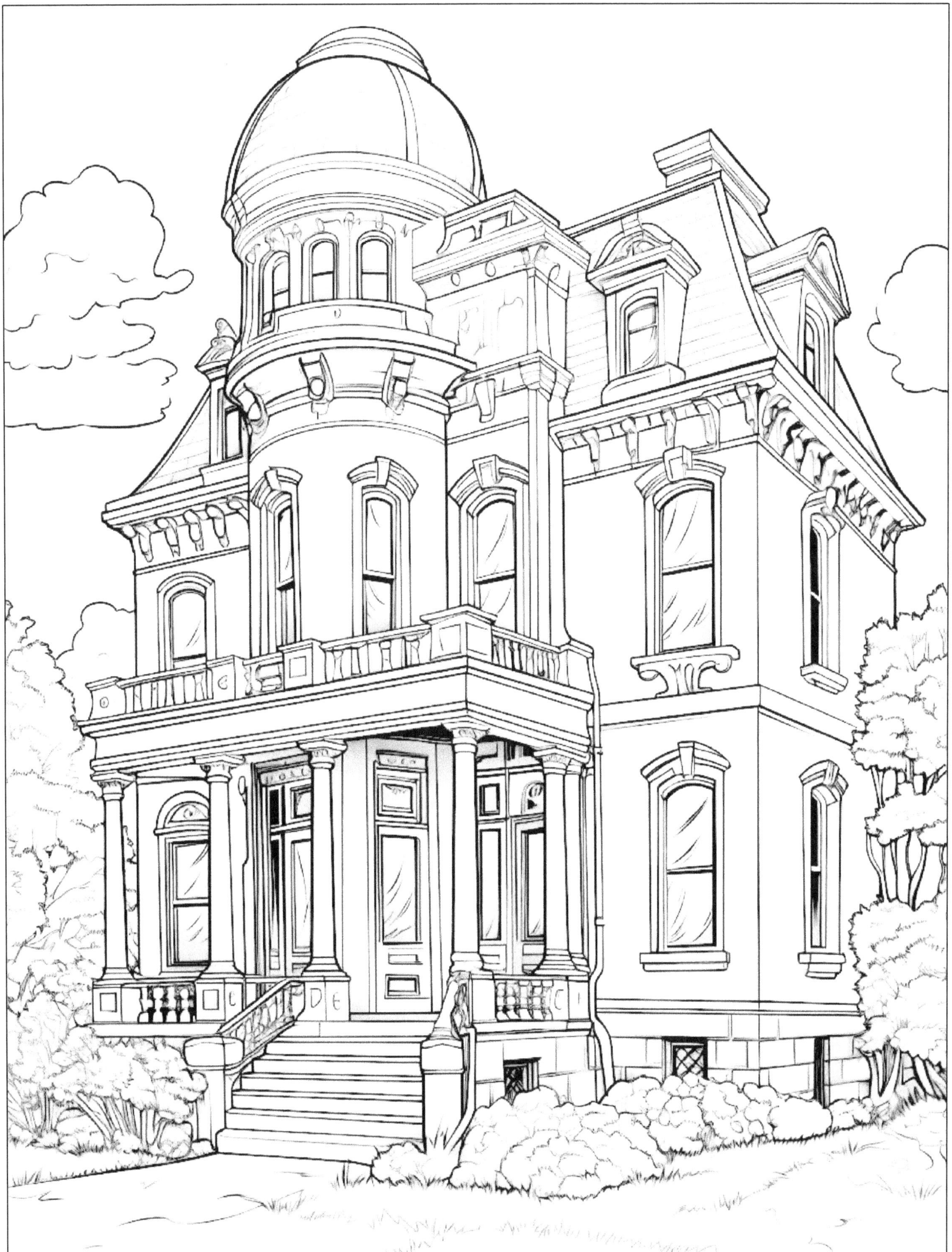

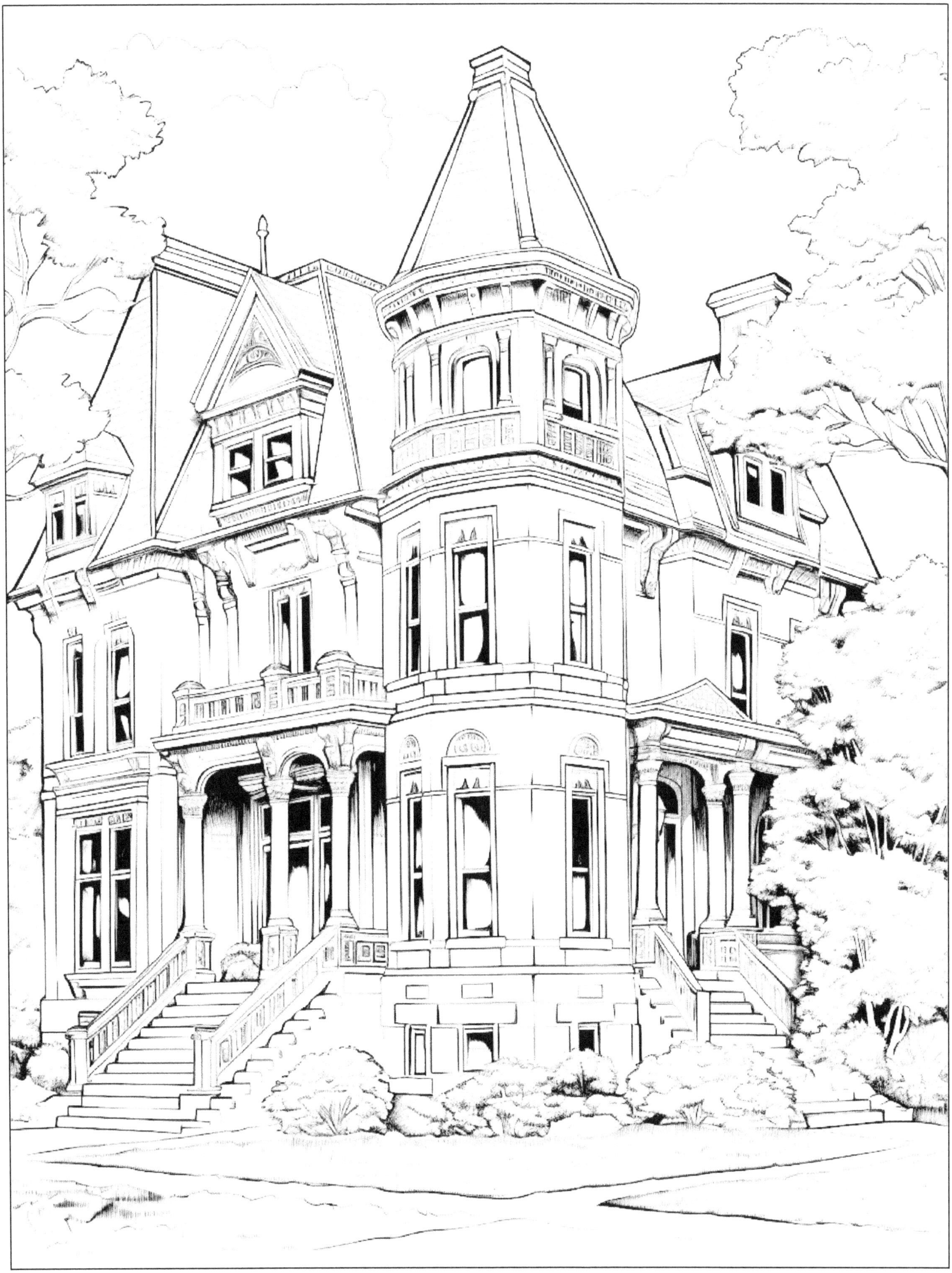

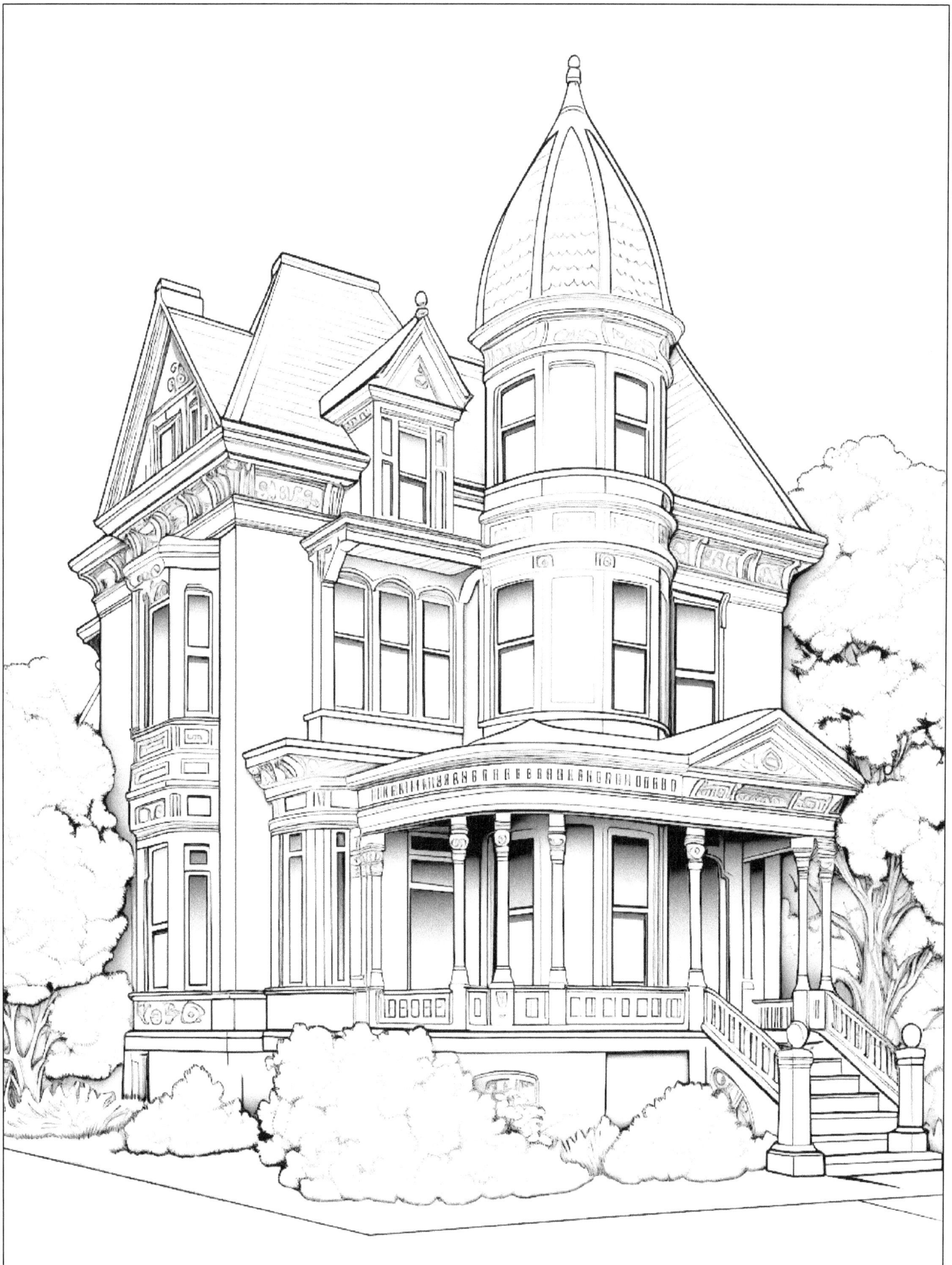

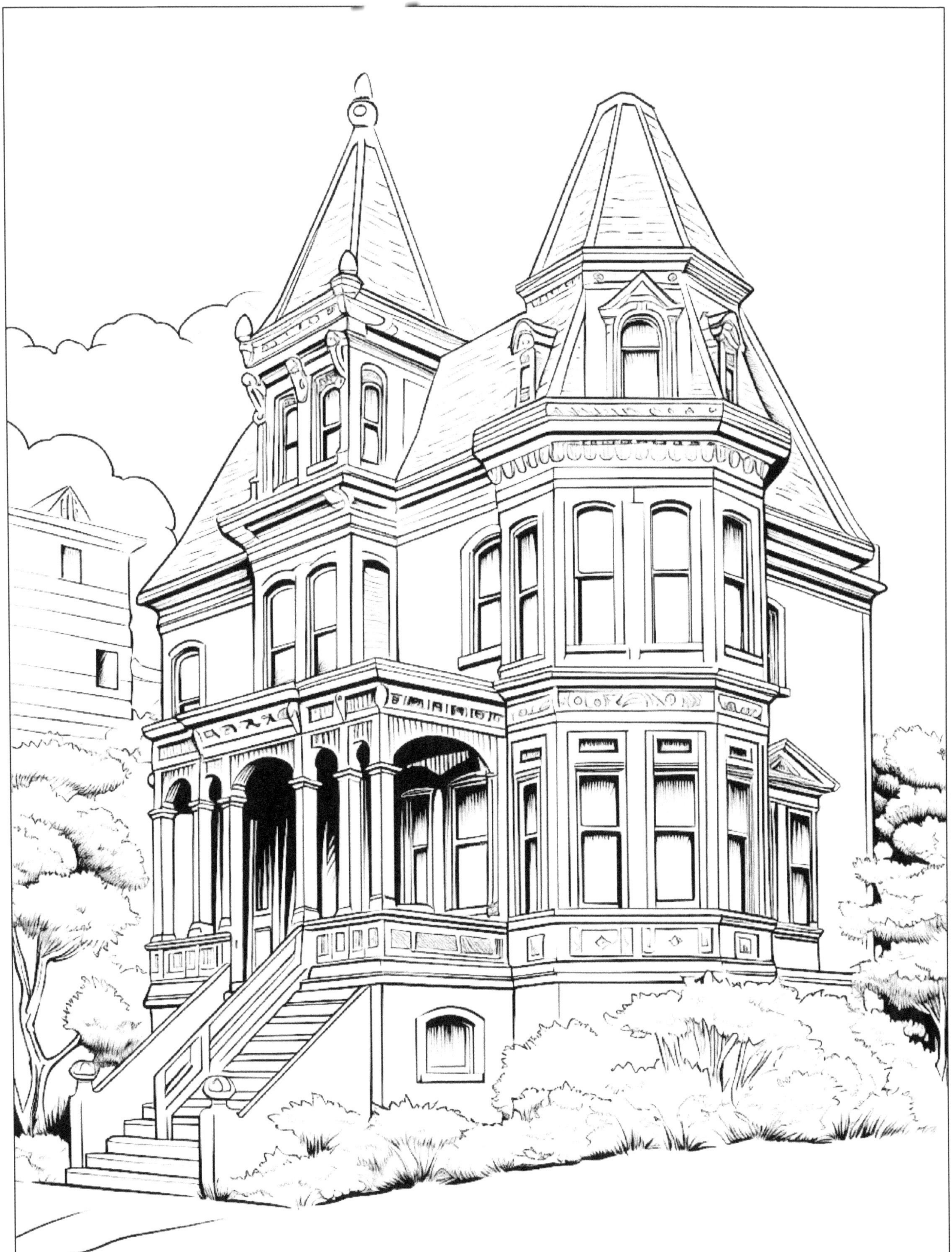

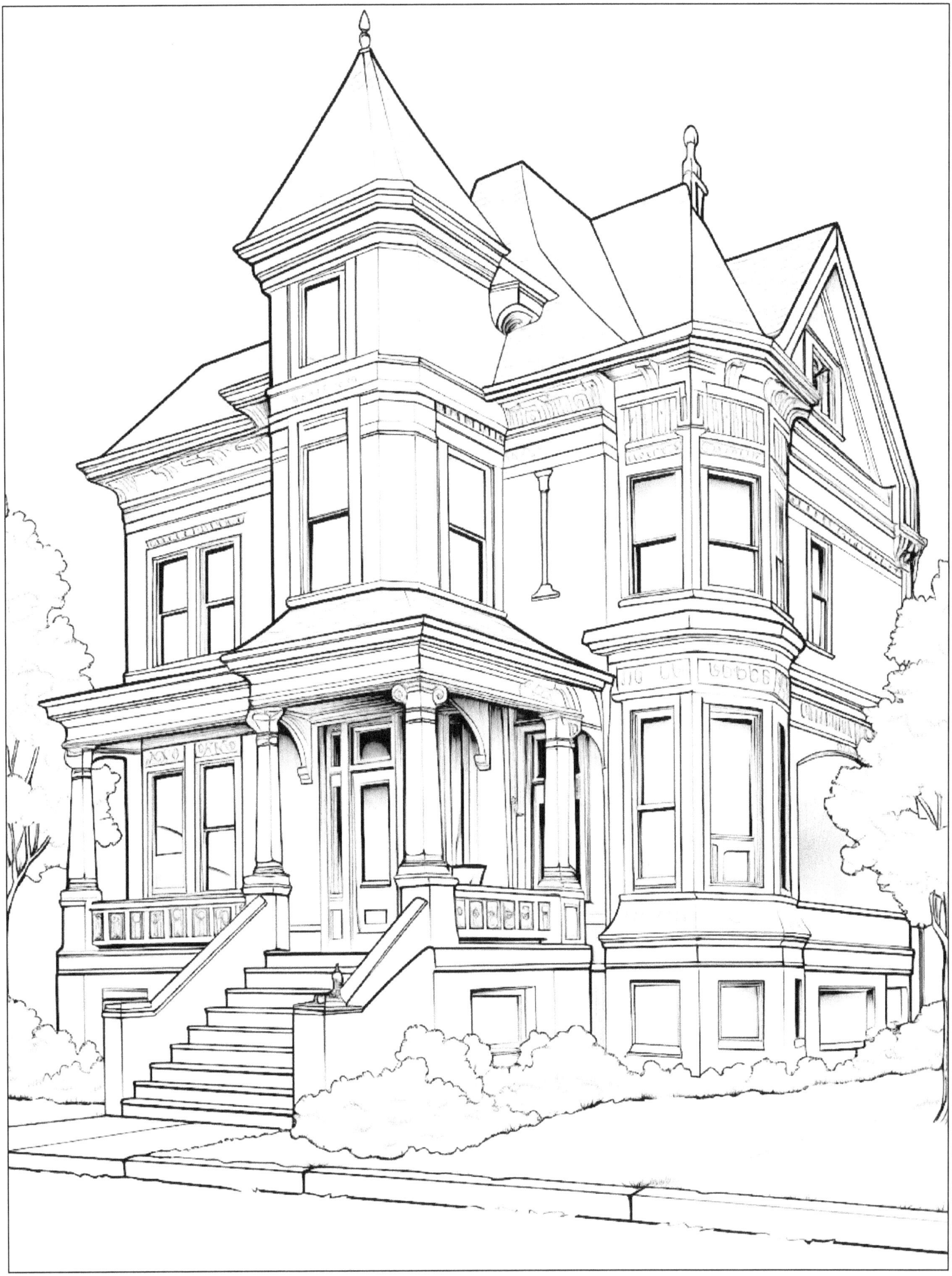

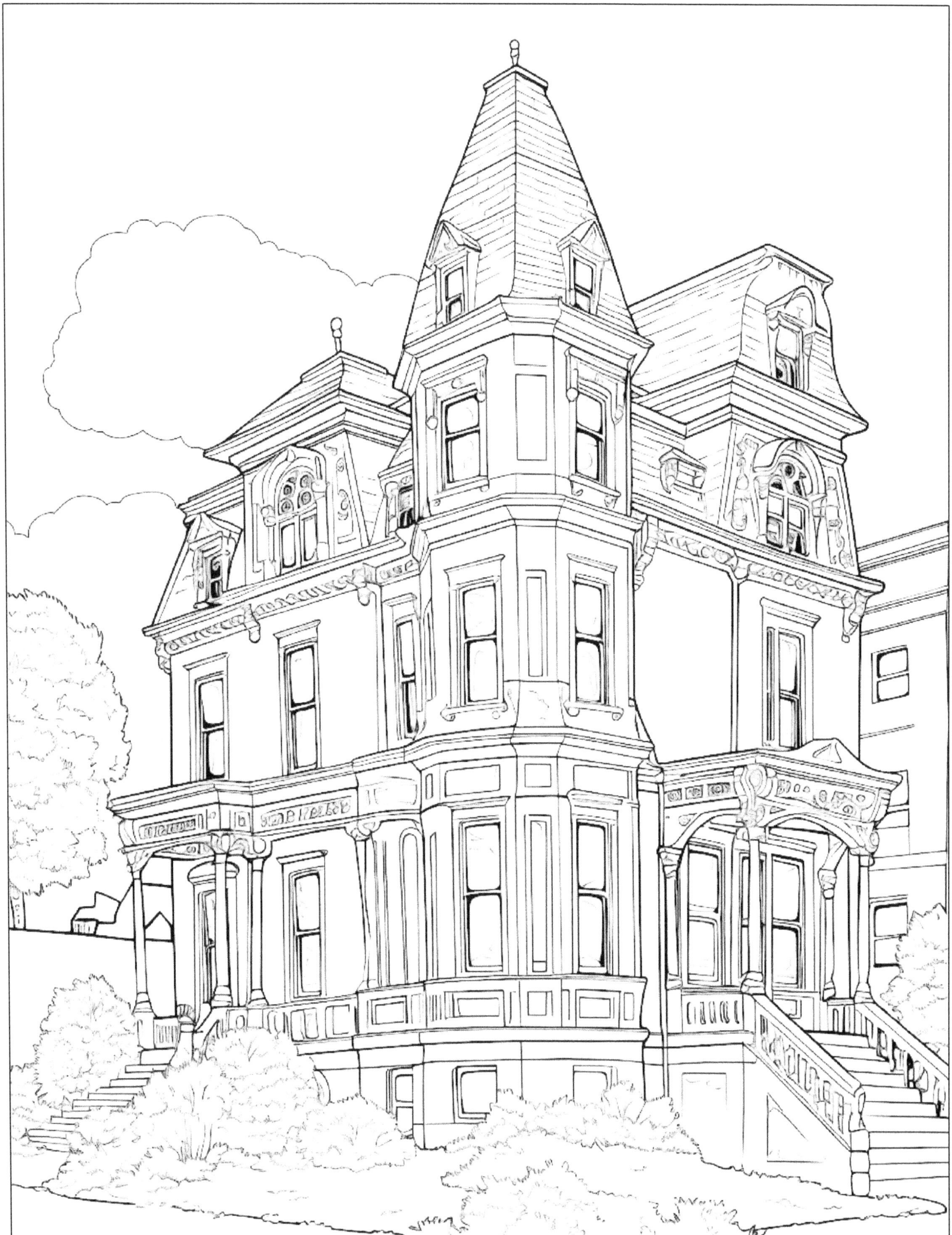

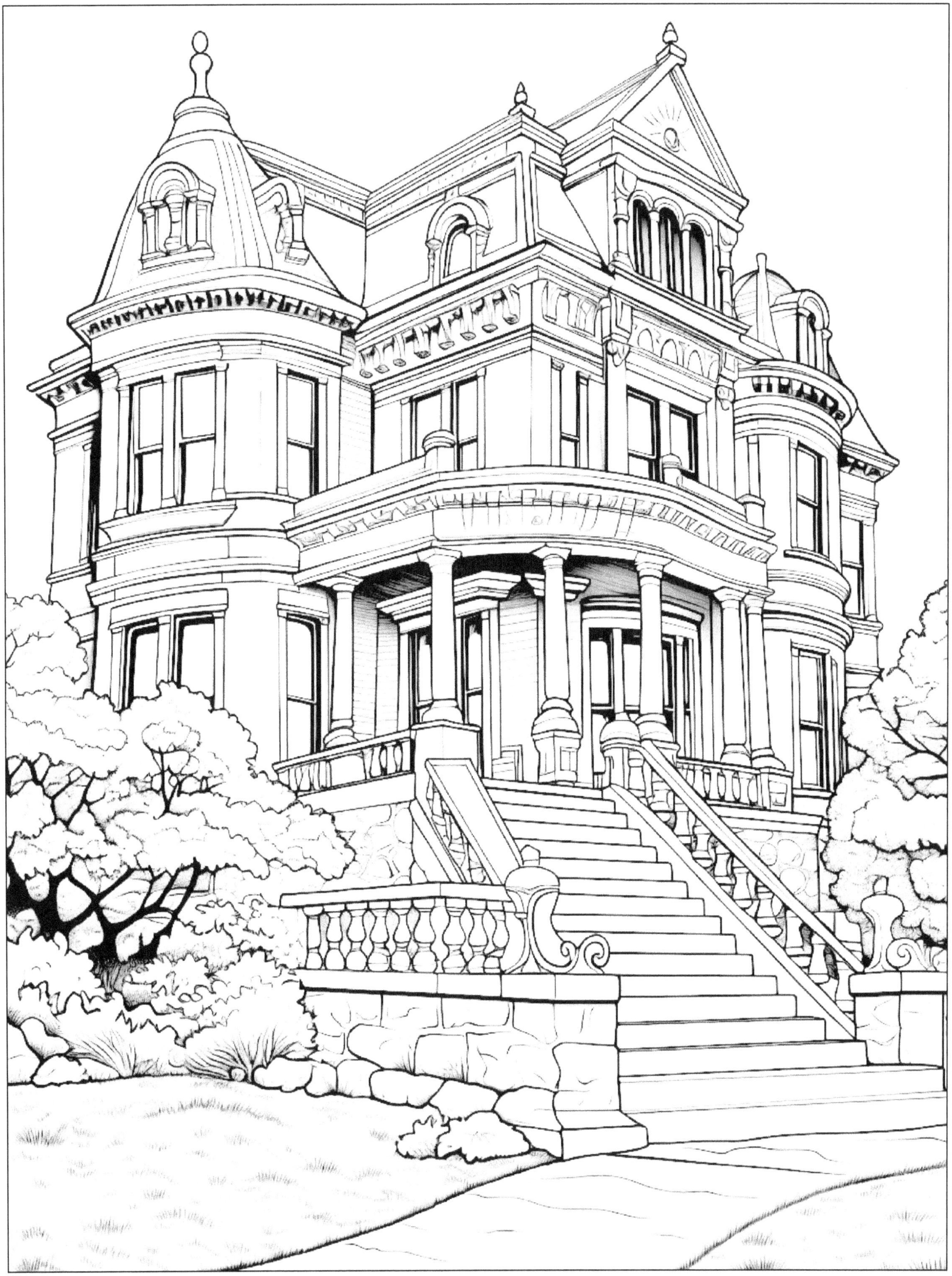

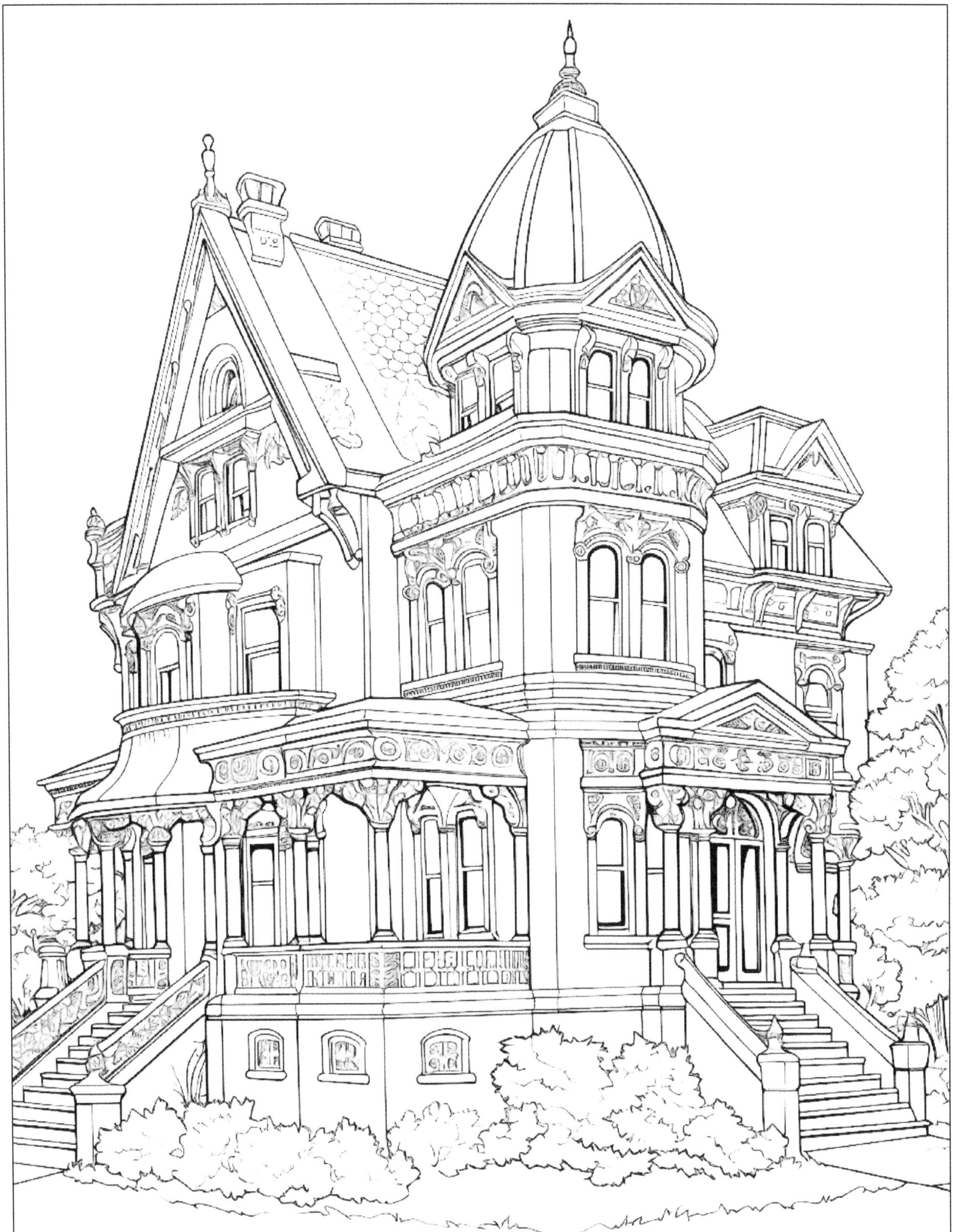

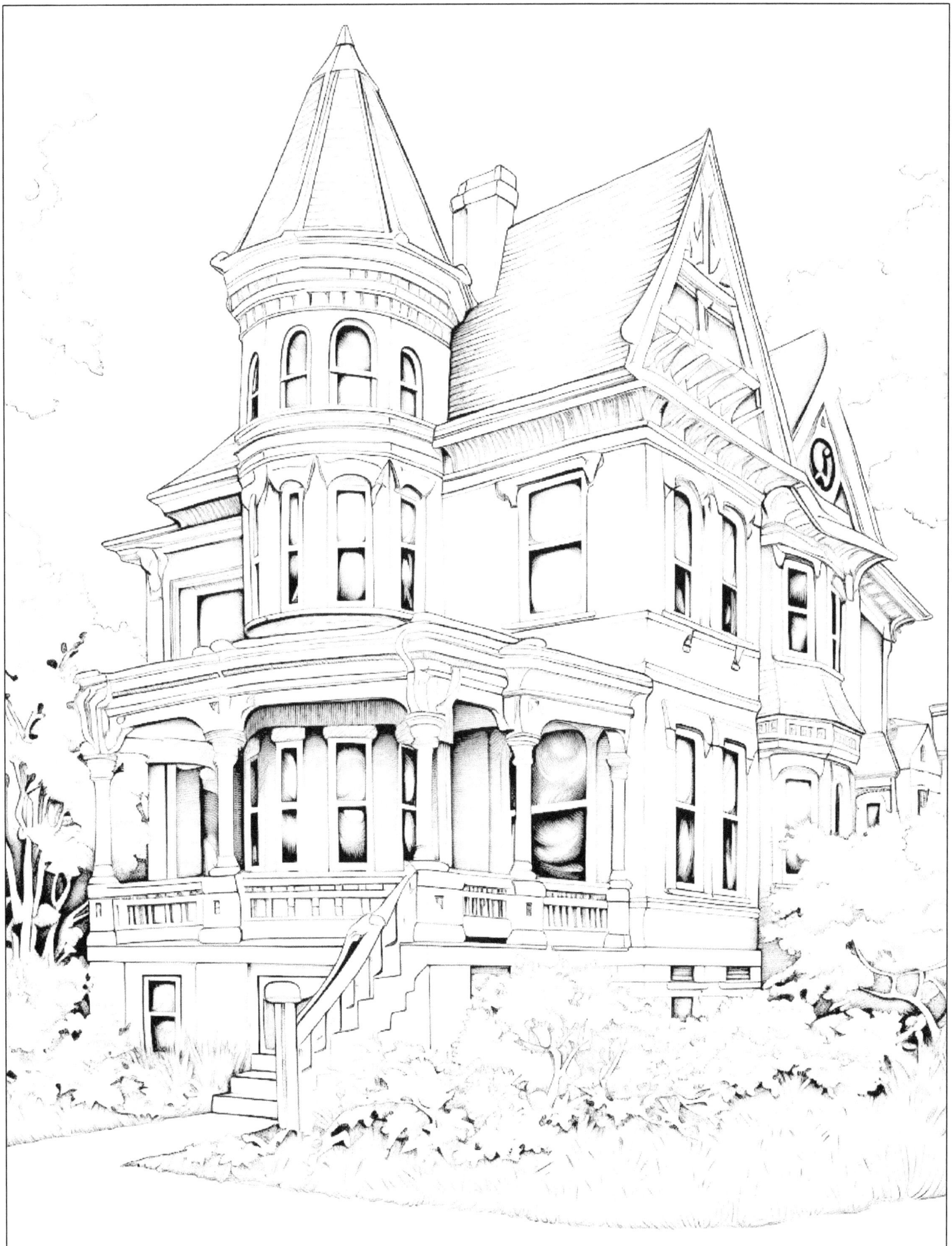

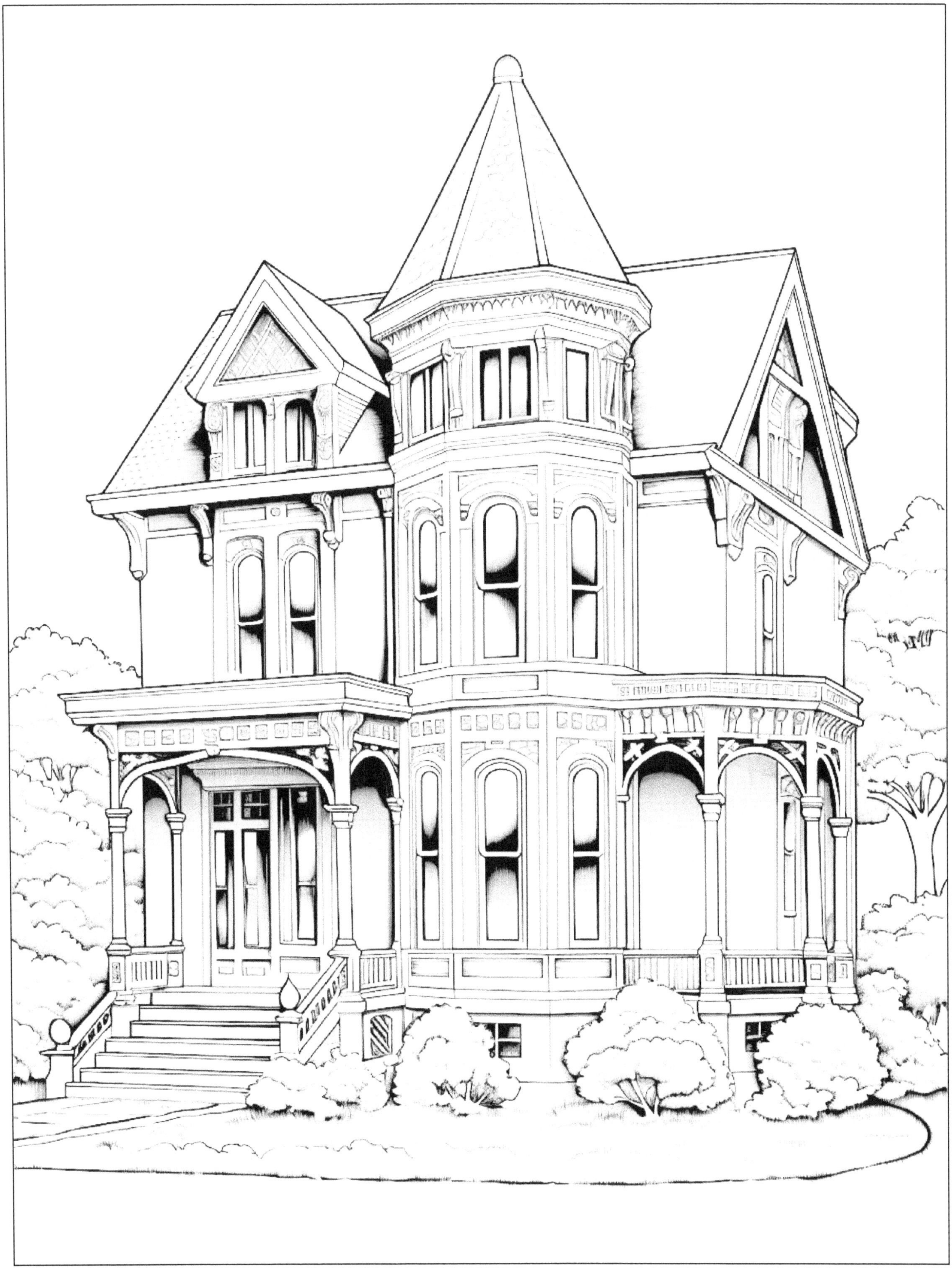

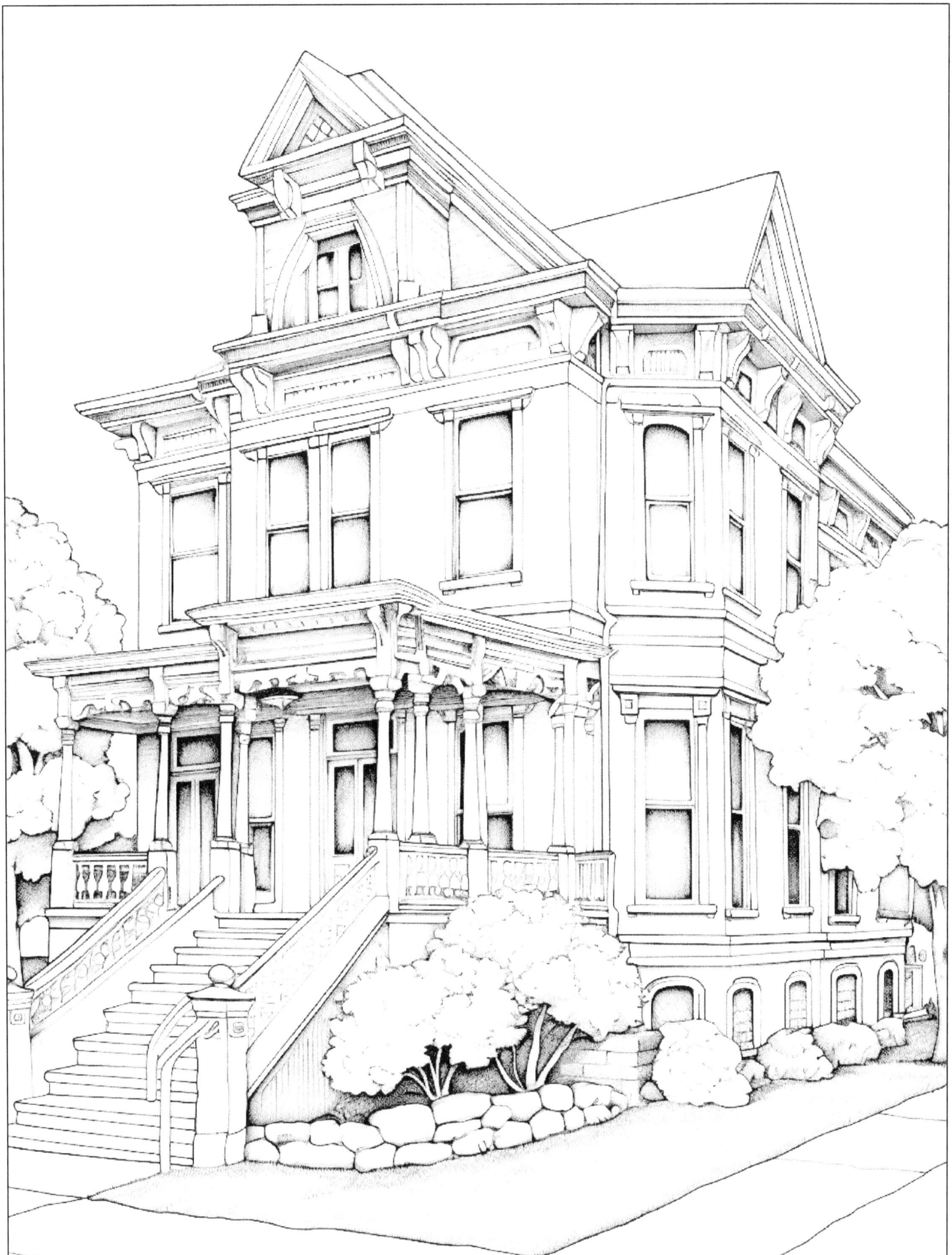

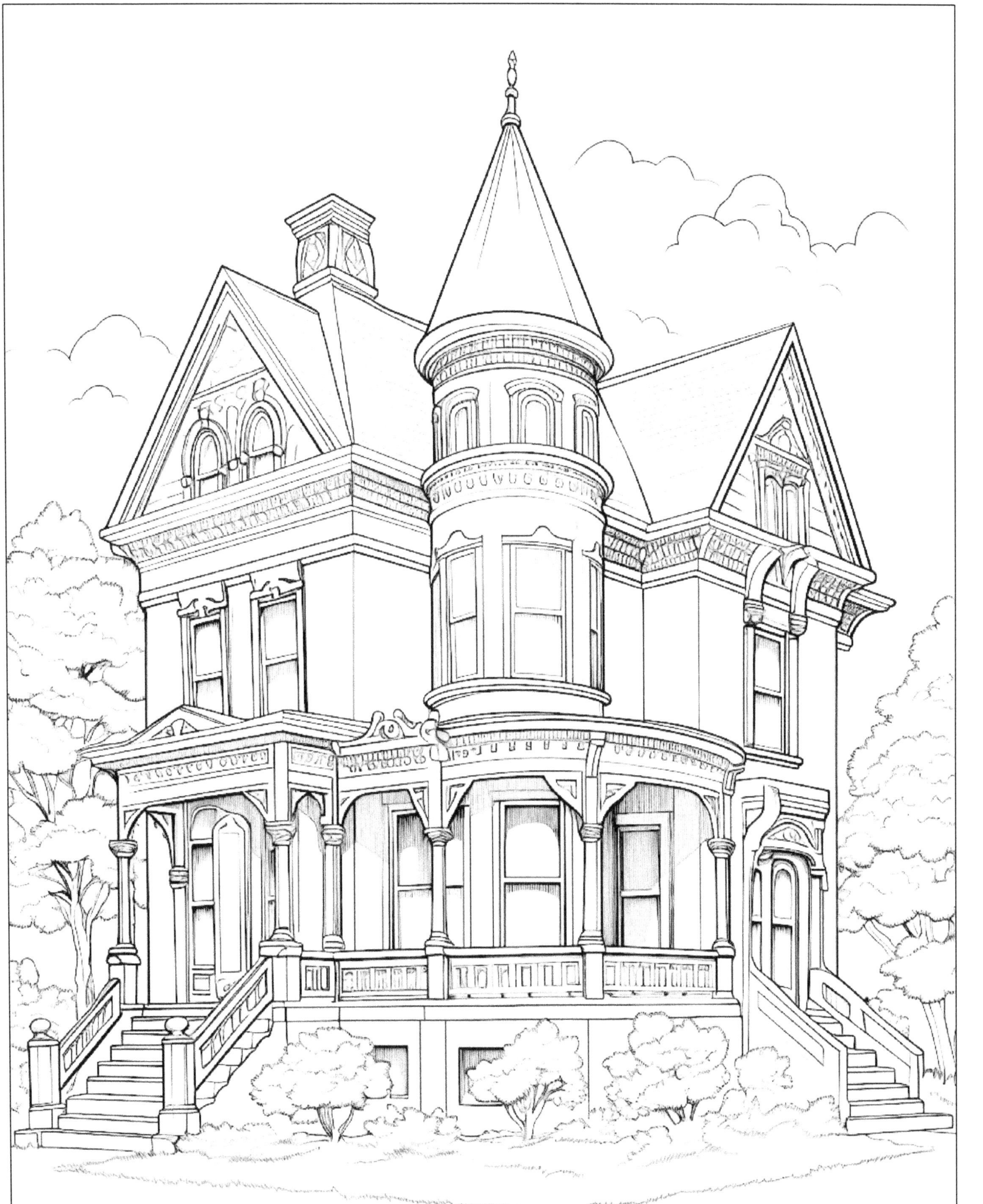

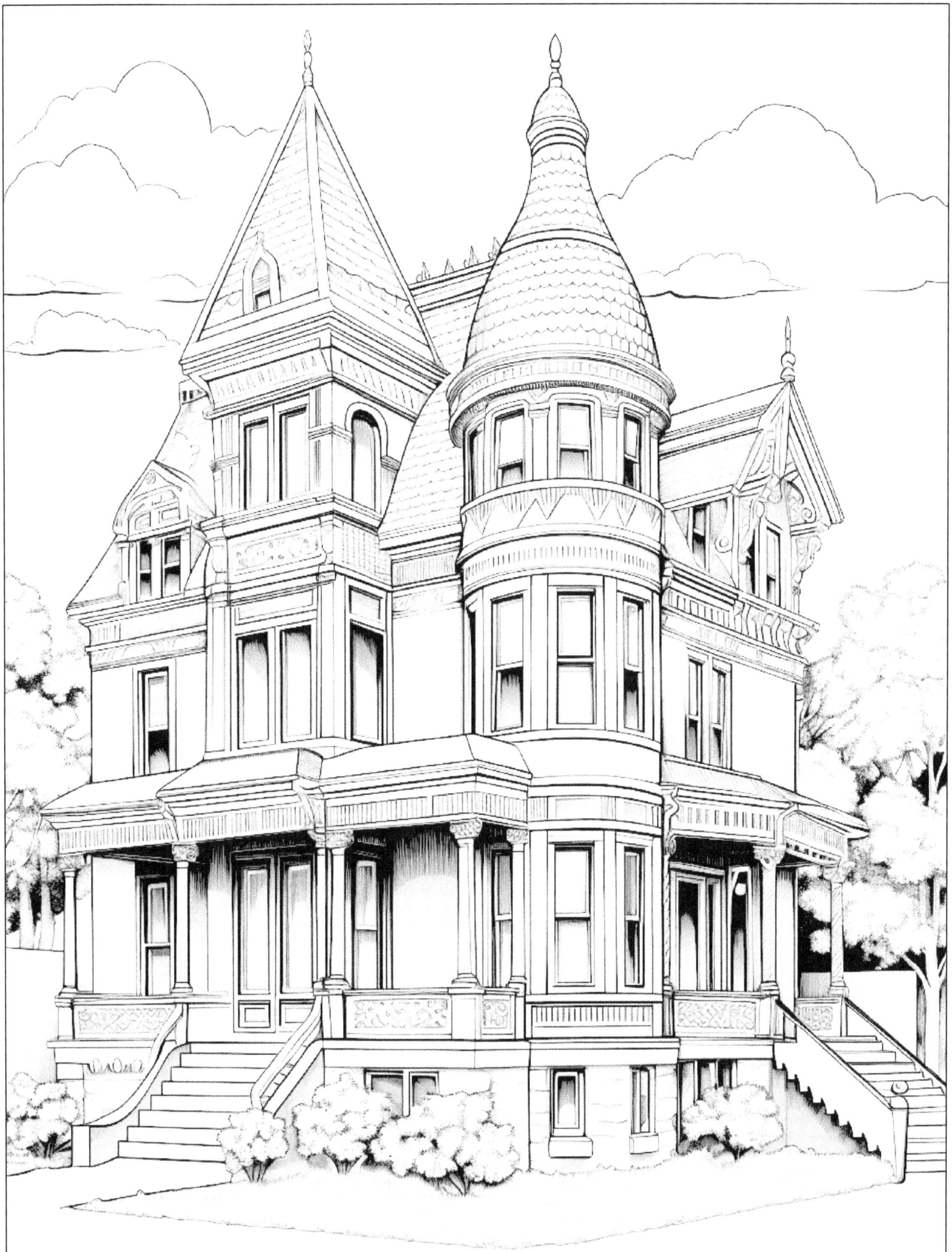

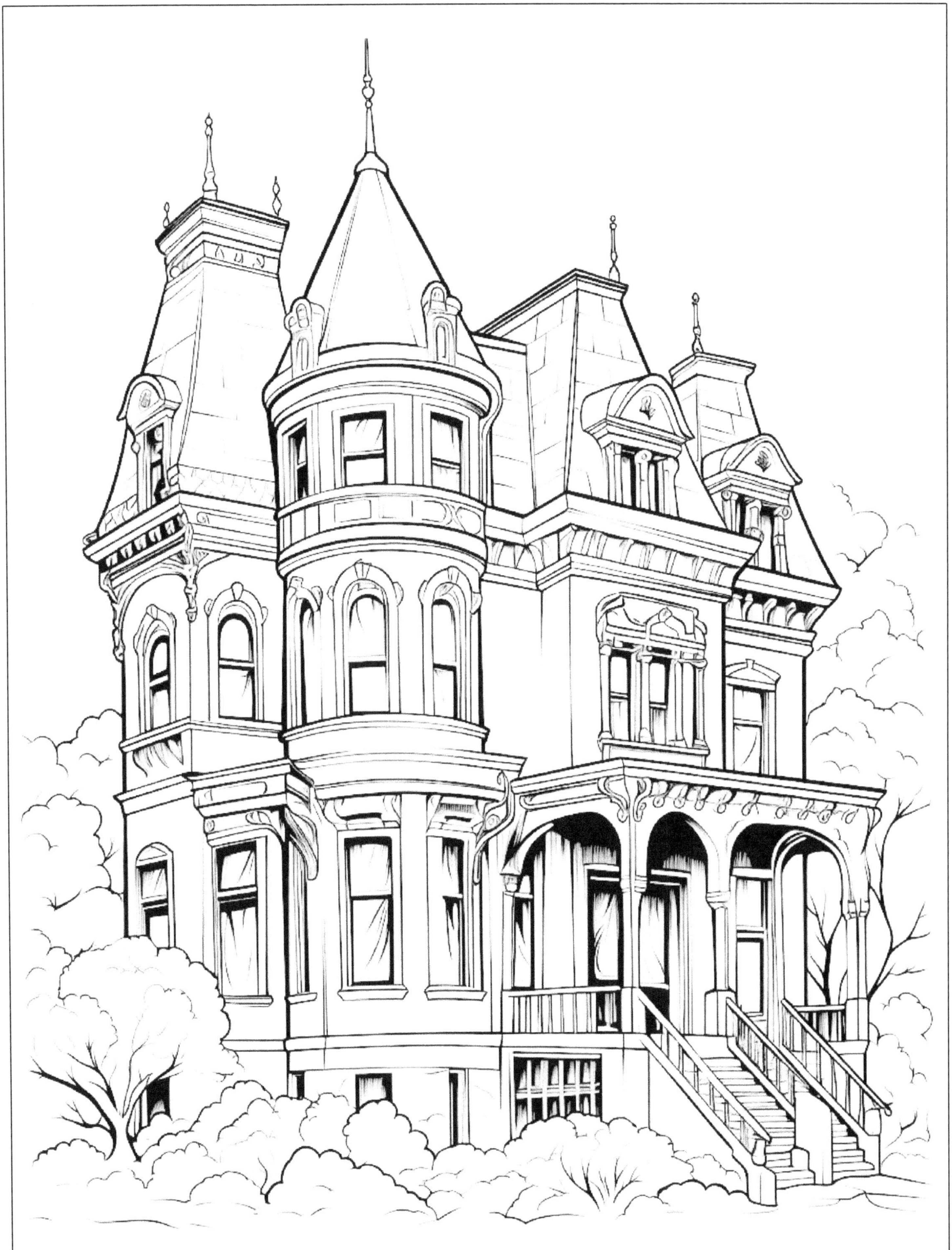

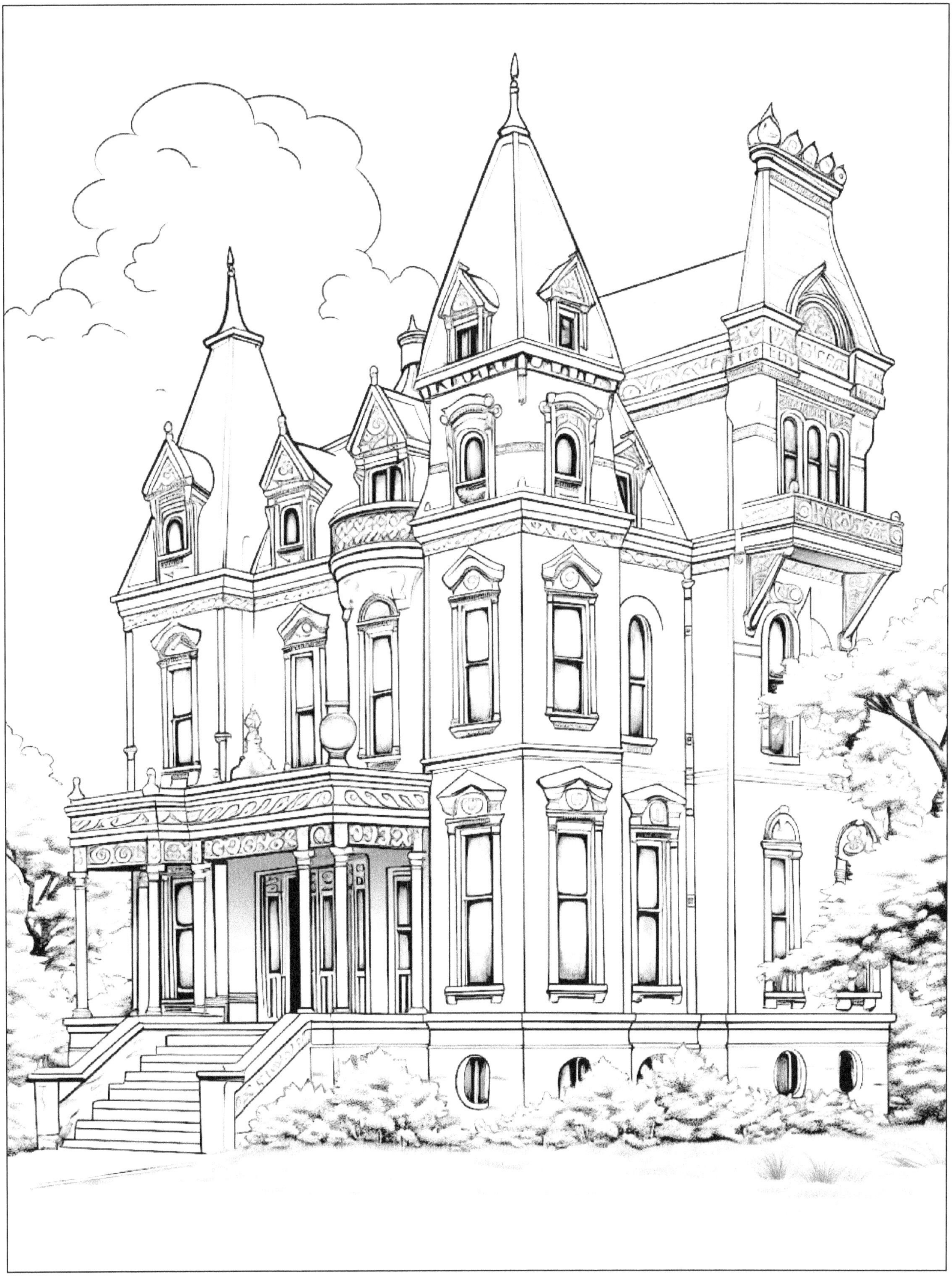

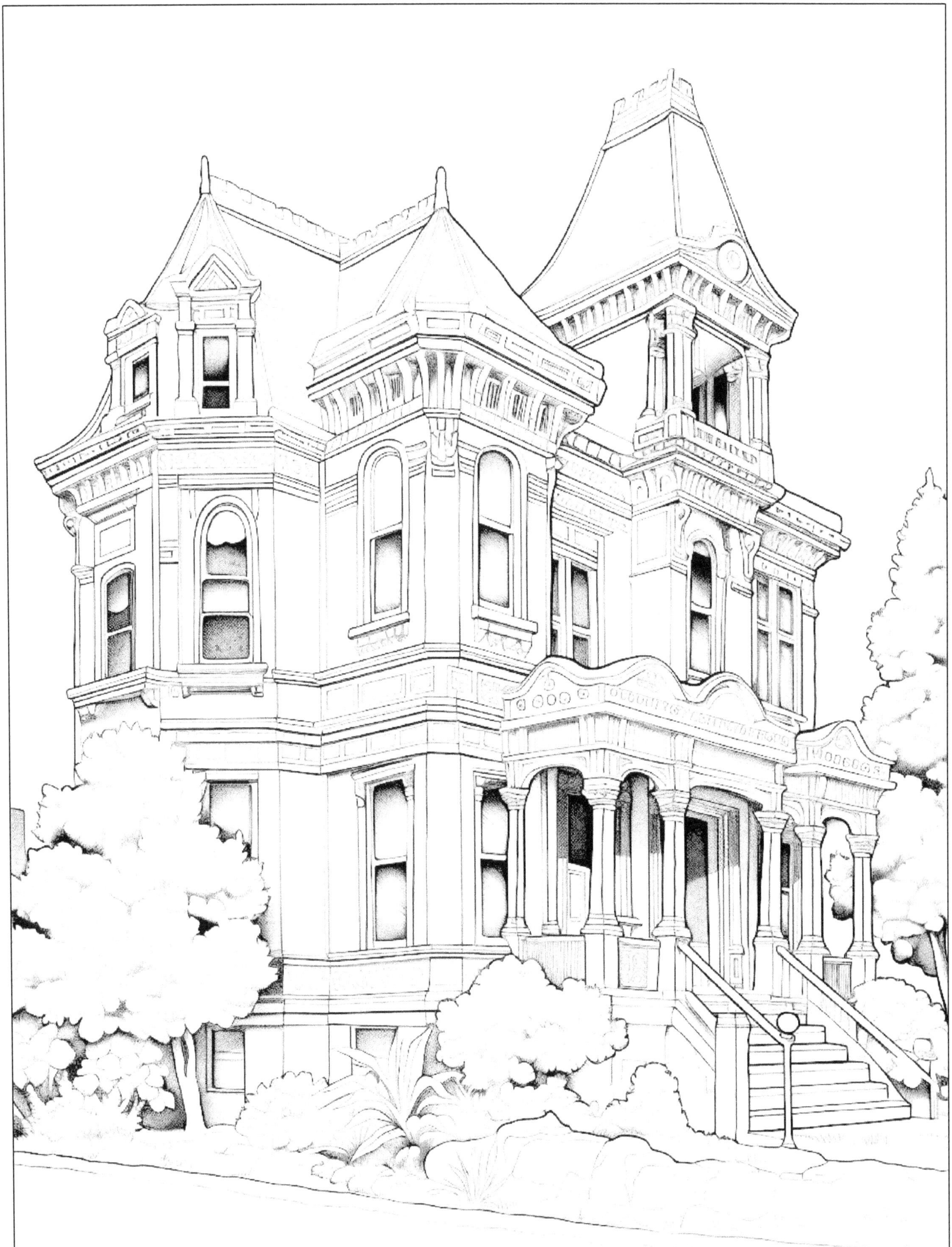

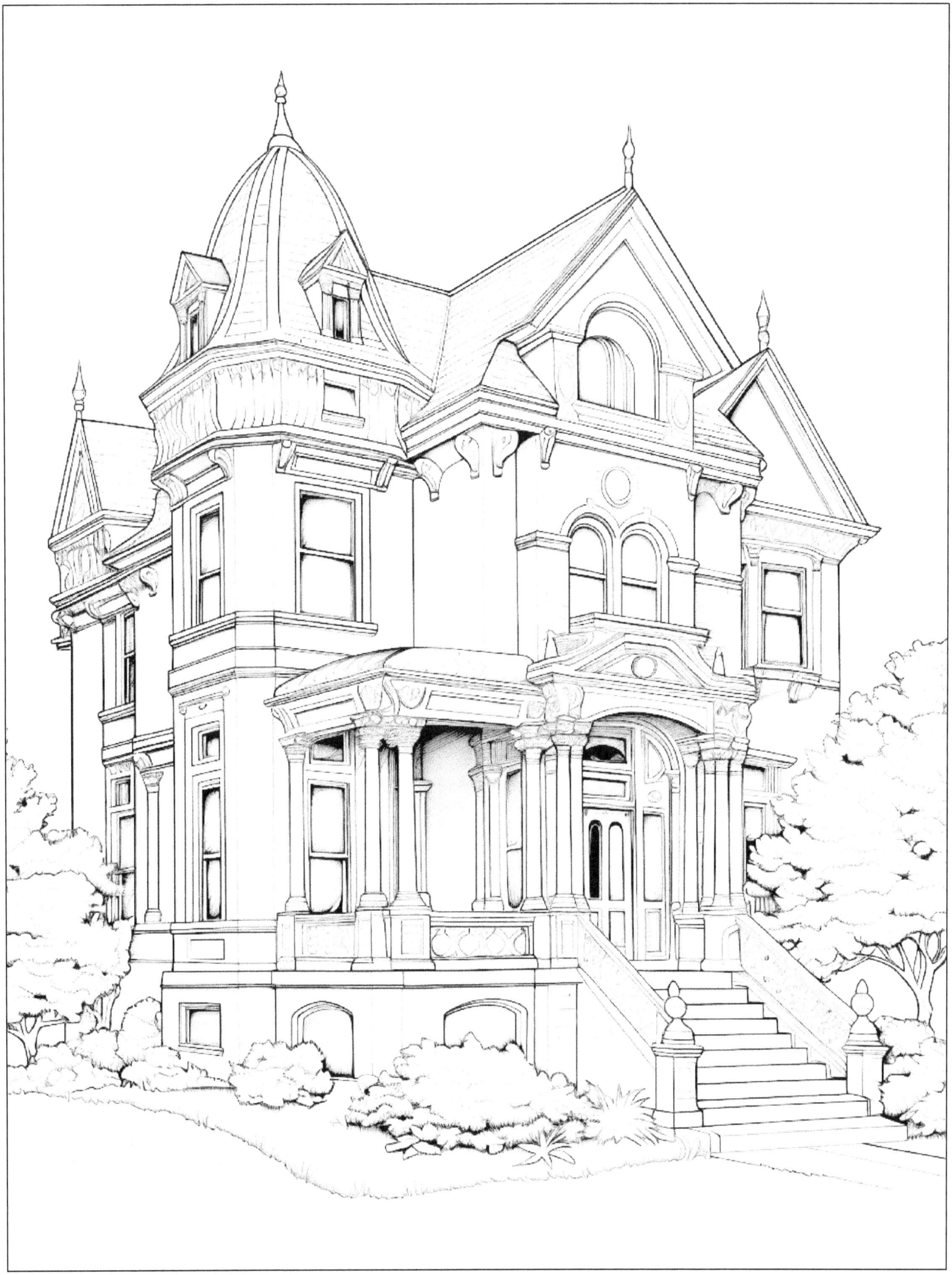

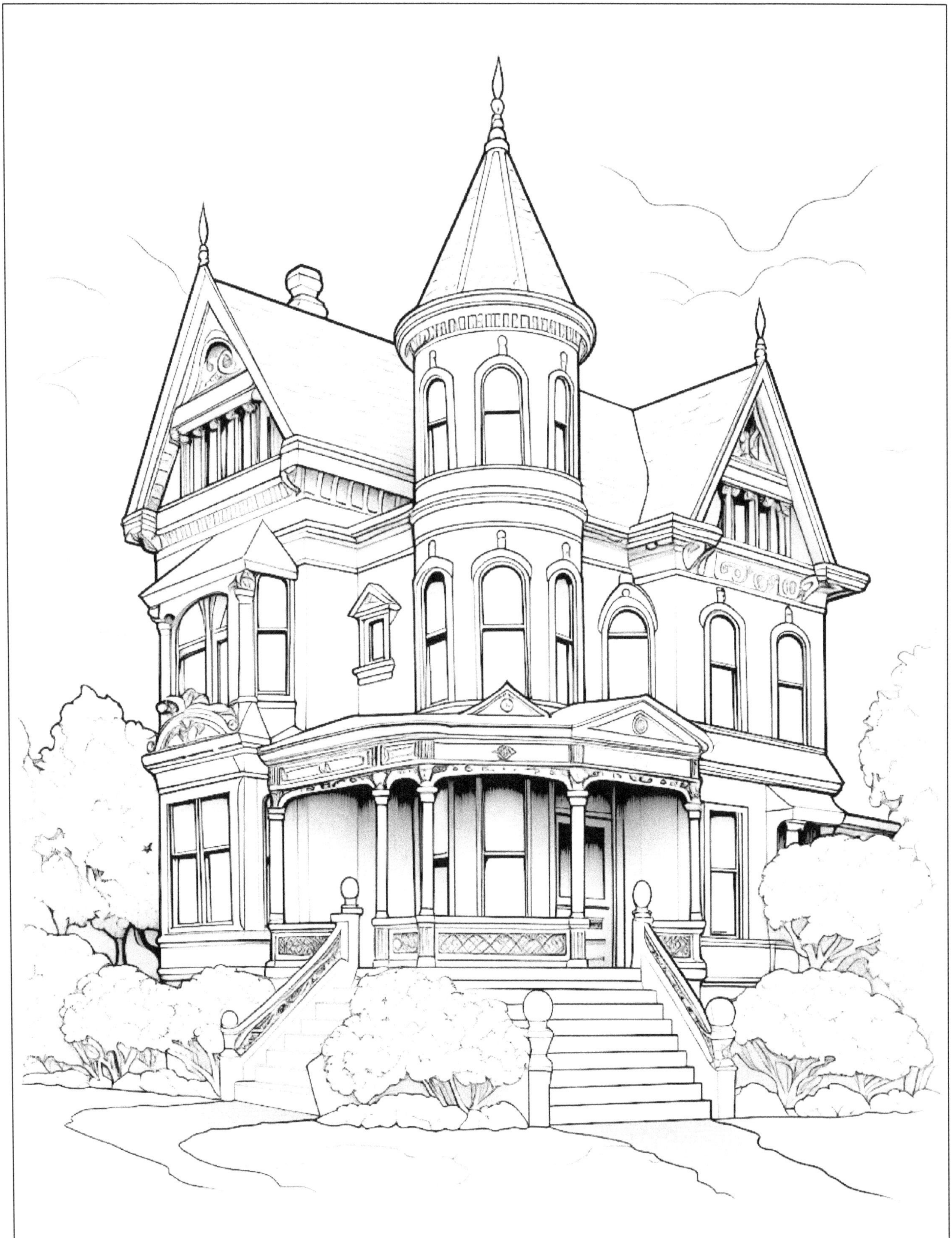

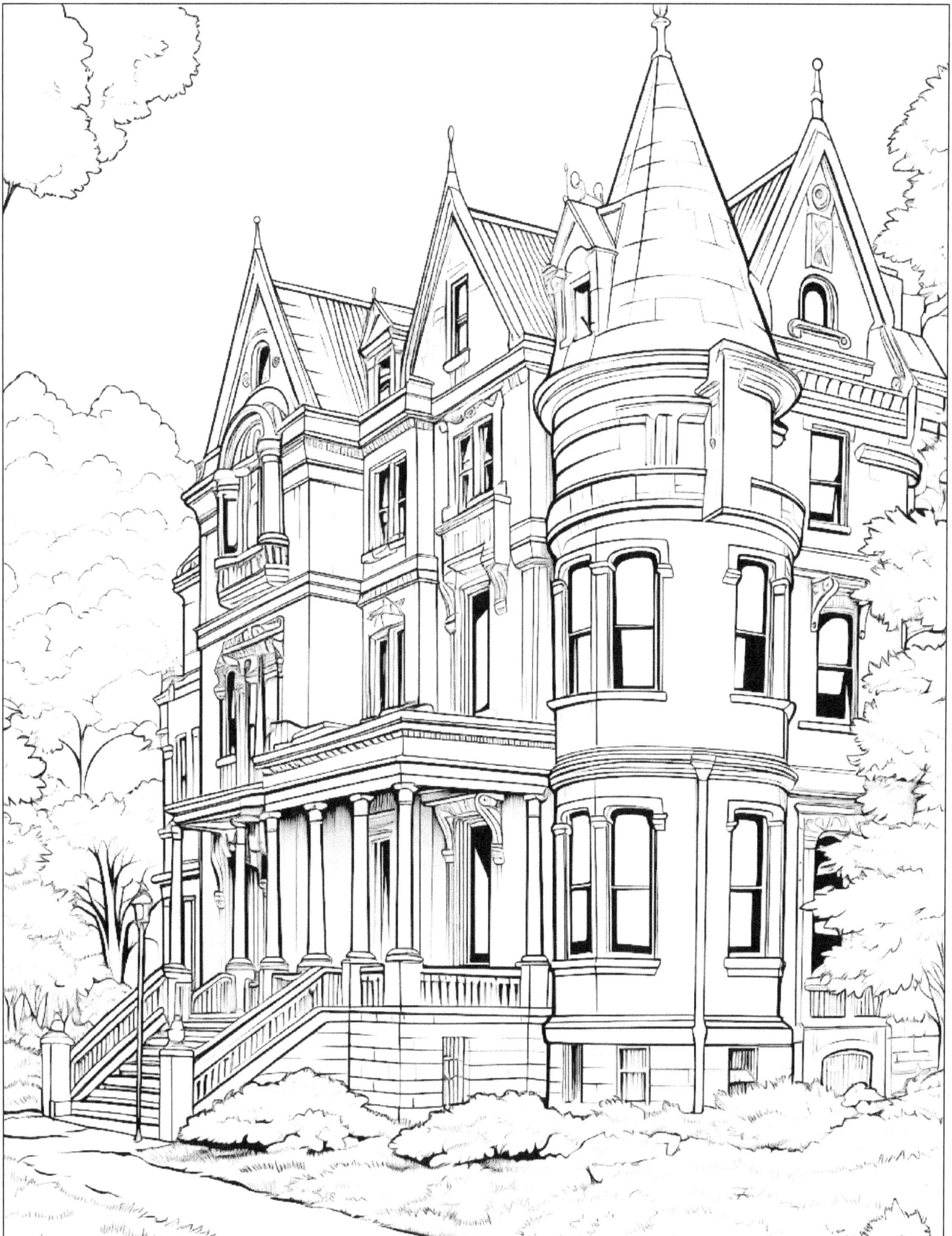

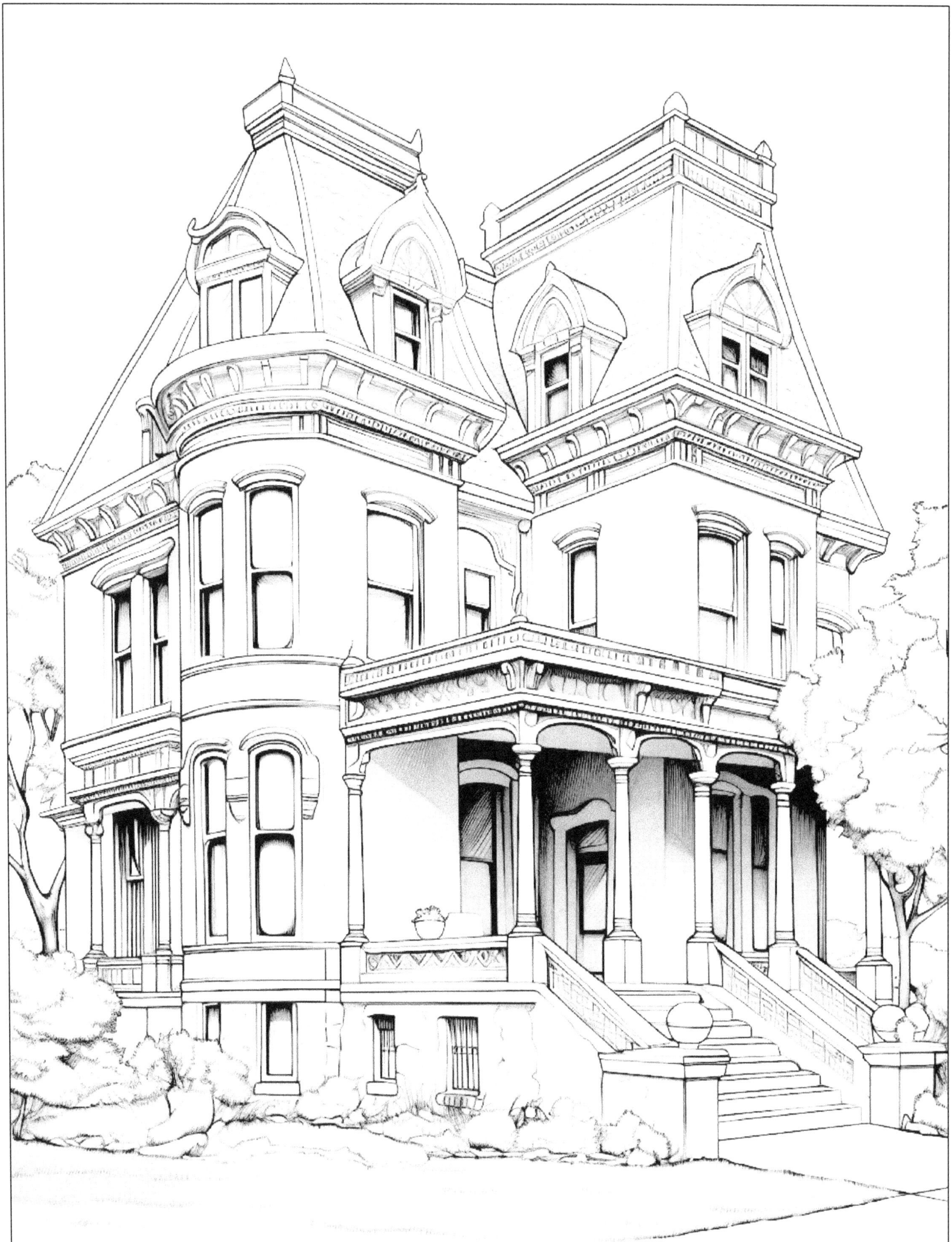

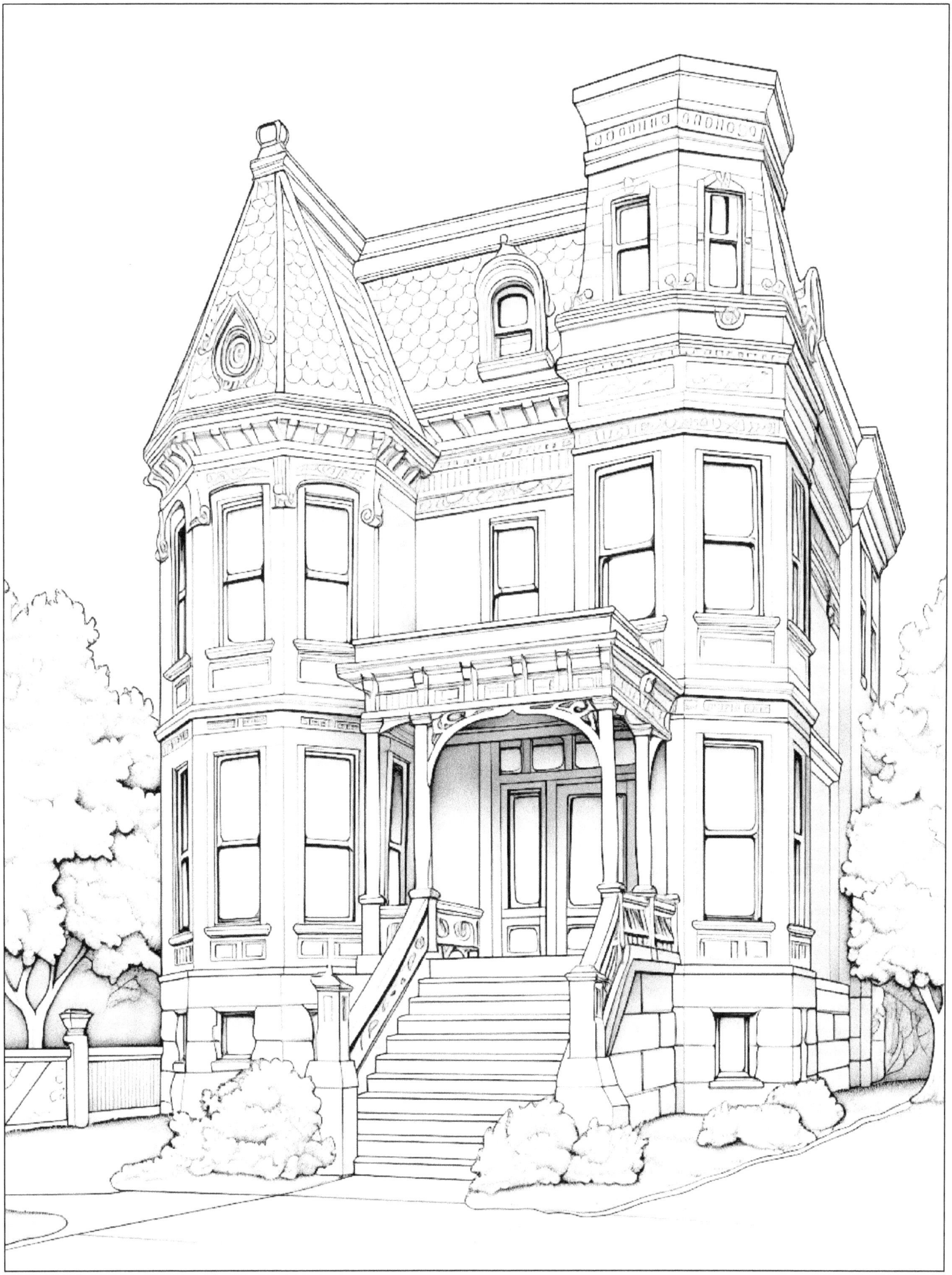

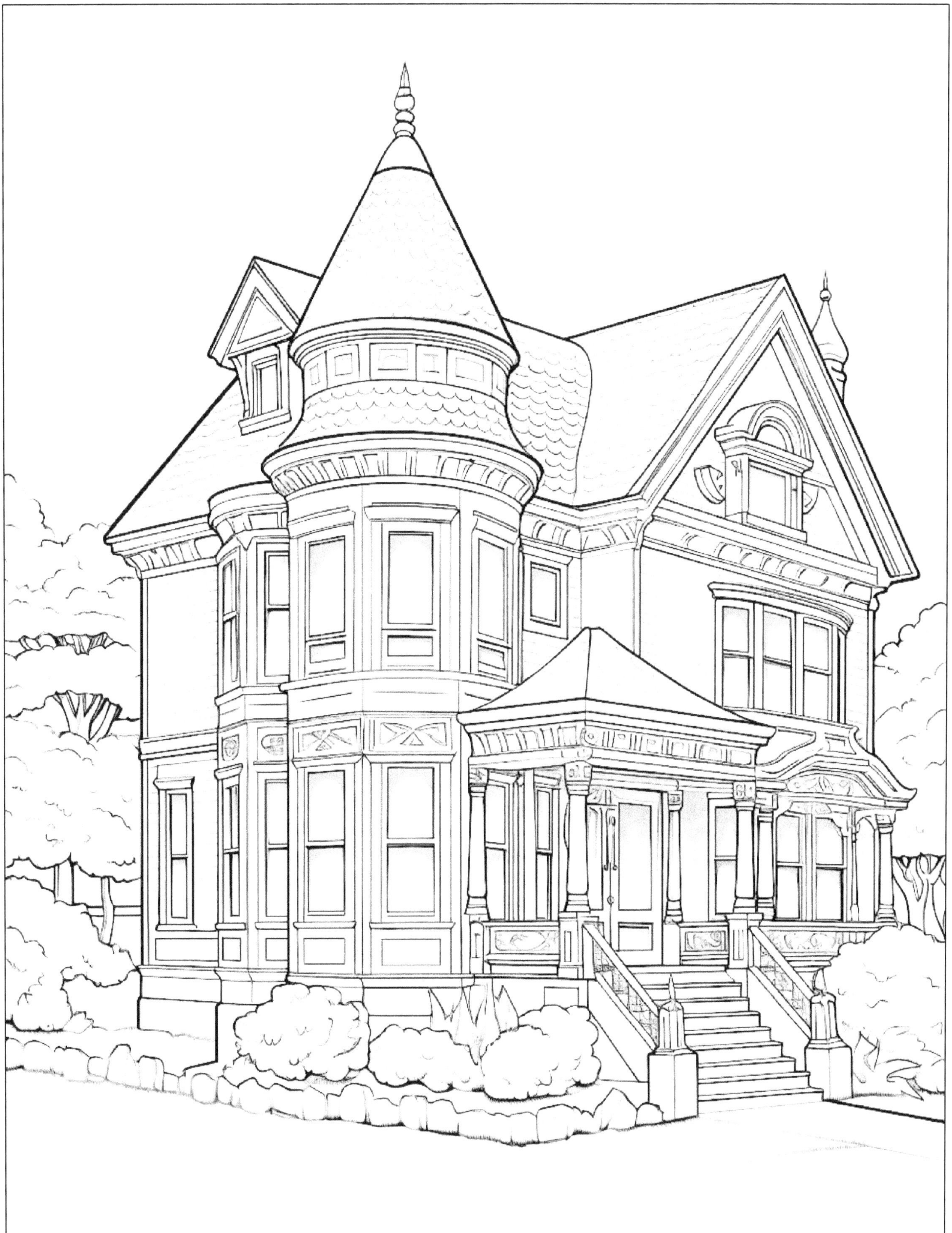

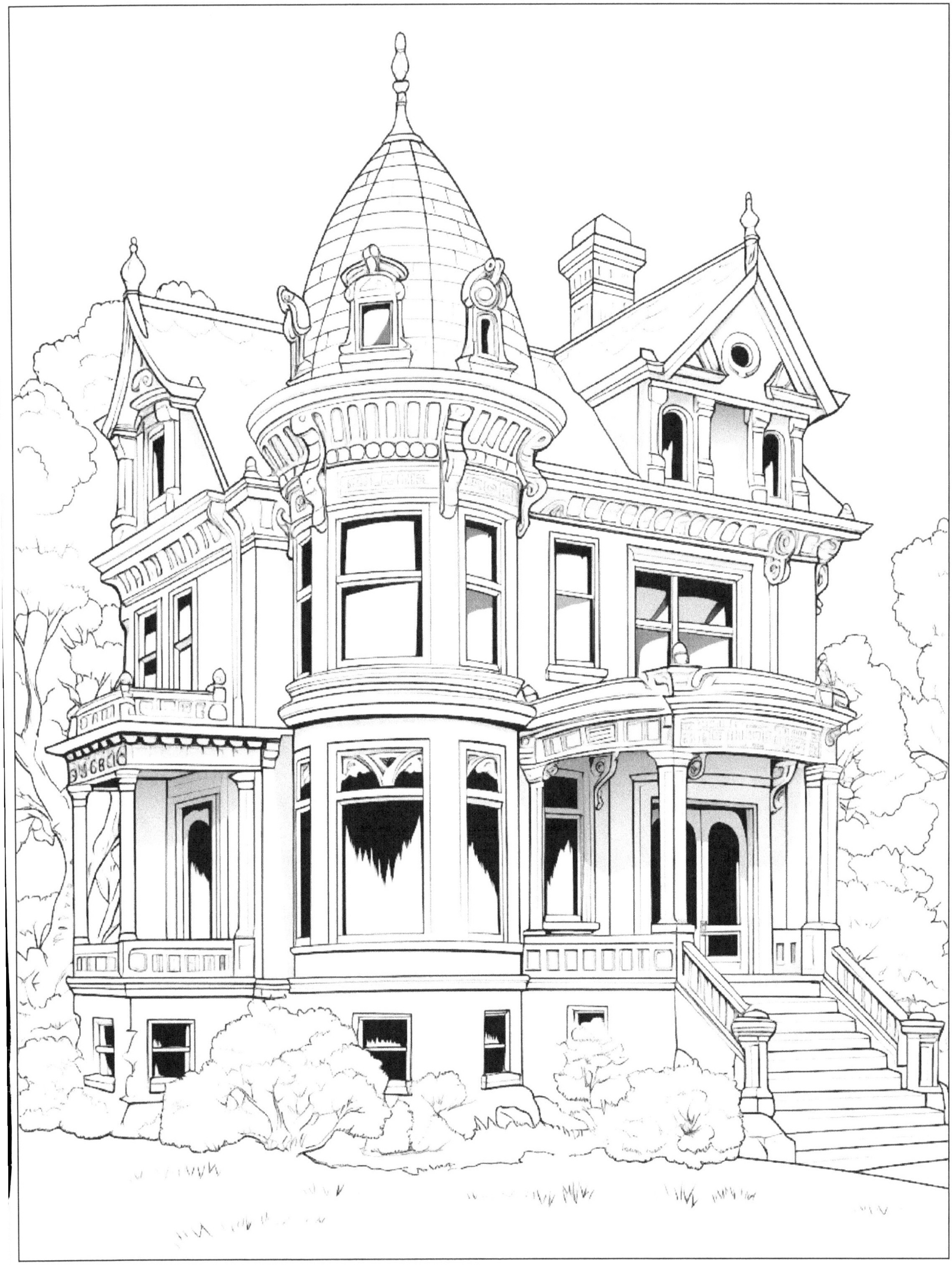

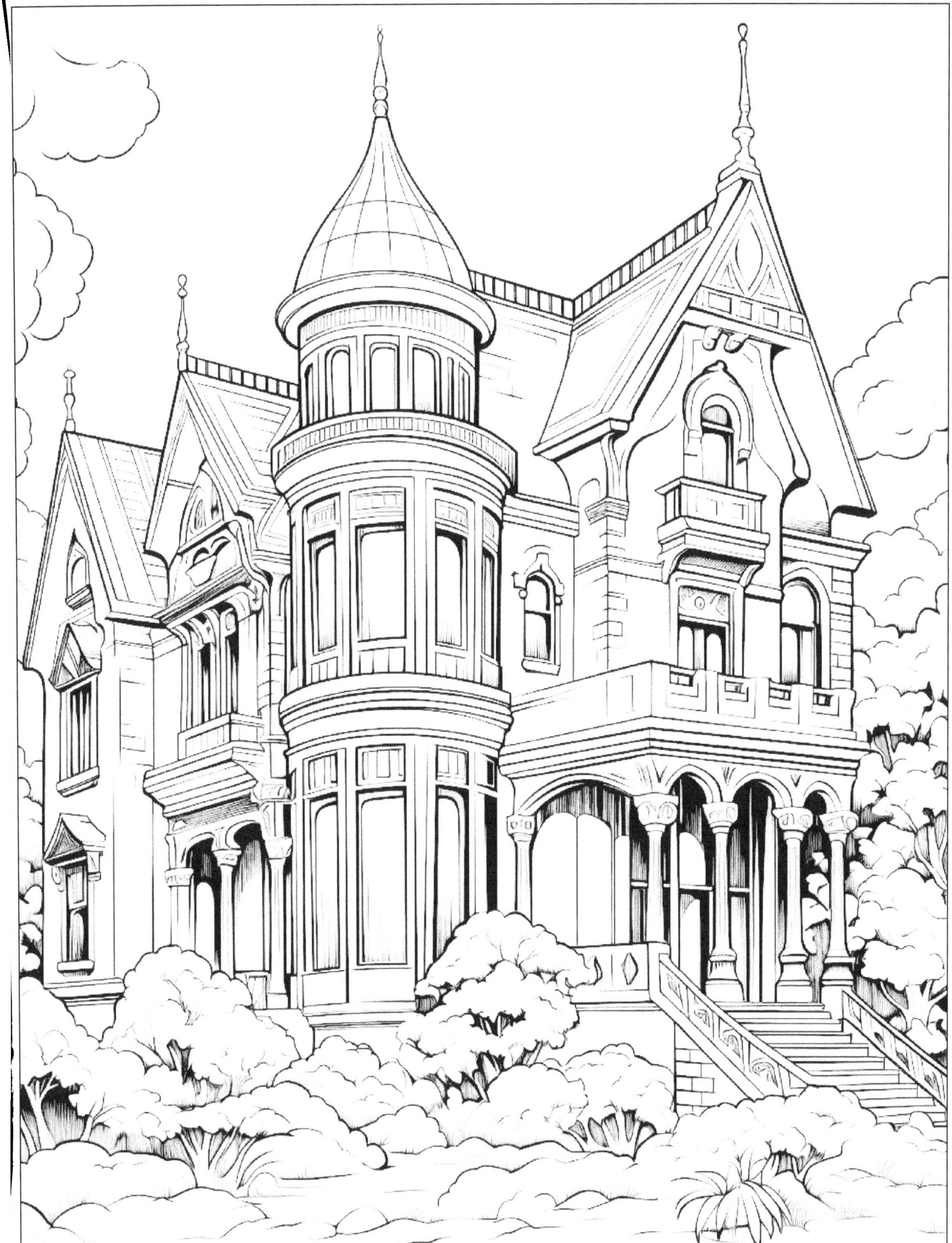

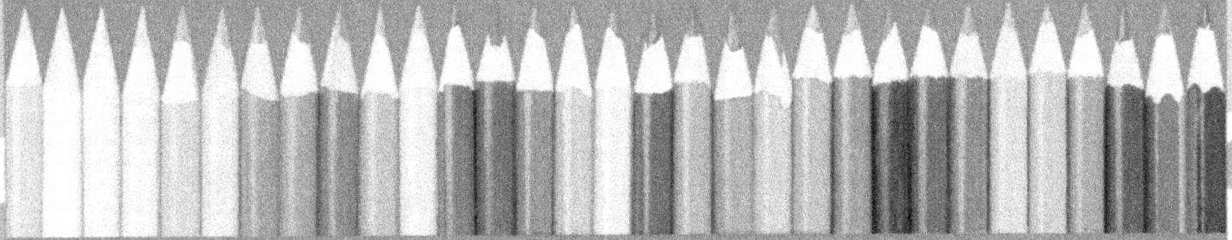

www.ingramcontent.com/pod-product-compliance
Lightning Source LLC
Chambersburg PA
CBHW062114220526
45471CB00010B/3731
* 9 7 9 8 3 2 3 2 7 3 8 3 6 *